Edgar Allan Poe

Literature and Life: American Writers

Selected list of titles in this series:

Complete list of titles in the series available from the publisher on request.

Edgar Allan POE

Bettina L. Knapp

A Frederick Ungar Book
CONTINUUM • NEW YORK

1990

Library of Congress Cataloging in Publication Data

Knapp, Bettina Liebowitz, 1926–
  Edgar Allan Poe.

  (Literature and life series)
  Bibliography: p.
  Includes index.
    1. Poe, Edgar Allen, 1809–1849. 2. Authors, American—
19th century—Biography. I. Title. II. Series.
PS2631.K58 1984   818'.309 [B]   84-4555
ISBN 0-8044-2476-4

Contents

Chronology

1809   Edgar Allan Poe is born in Boston on January 19 to actors, Elizabeth Arnold Poe and David Poe who deserts mother and son.

1811   After mother's death, Edgar is taken into the home of John and Frances Allan of Richmond.

1815   Sails with the Allans to England, where he attends various schools.

1820   When John Allan's business begins to fail they return to Richmond.

1825   John Allan inherits a large sum of money.

1826   Becomes engaged to Sarah Elmira Royster. Enrolls at the University of Virginia. Leaves in December after having incurred some debts. Estrangement between himself and John Allan.

1827   Because he is unable to pay his debts, Poe runs away to Boston and enlists in the army. Publishes *Tamerlane and Other Poems*. Sarah marries A. B. Shelton.

1829   Frances Allan dies. Poe requests and receives an Honorable Discharge. *Al Aaraaf, Tamerlane, and Minor Poems* published in Baltimore. Temporary reconciliation with John Allan.

1830   Writes "To Helen." Enters West Point. John Allan remarries. Severs relations with Poe.

1831   Arranges to be dismissed from West Point. Publishes *Poems*. Writes "Israfel" and *Tales of the Folio Club*. Moves to Baltimore.

1833   Wins a 50-dollar prize from the *Baltimore Saturday Visitor* with his "MS. Found in a Bottle."

1834   John Allan dies. He leaves nothing to Poe.

1835   Begins writing review for *Southern Literary Messenger* in Richmond. Secretly marries his thirteen-year-old cousin, Virginia Clemm.

1836   Remarries Virginia publicly.

1837   Writes *The Narrative of Arthur Gordon Pym*.

1838   Moves to Philadelphia.

1839   Writes "The Fall of the House of Usher." Takes job as Associate Editor of *Burton's Gentlemen's Magazine*. Arranges for the publication of *The Tales of the Grotesque and Arabesque*.

1841   Writes "The Murders in the Rue Morgue."
       His health grows steadily worse and his fi-
       nancial problems mount. He accepts editor-
       ship of *Graham's Magazine*. Completes "A
       Descent into the Maelstrom."

1842   Virginia bursts a blood vessel in her throat.
       She will live five more years. Leaves
       Graham's Magazine. Writes "The Oval Por-
       trait," "The Mystery of Marie Rogêt," and
       "The Masque of the Red Death.

1843   Reputation grows with the publication of
       "The Gold Bug" in the *Dollar Newspaper*.
       Publishes "The Tell-Tale Heart," "The Black
       Cat" and "The Pit and the Pendulum."

1844   Writes "The Purloined Letter." Moves to
       New York. Publishes "The Raven," which
       makes him famous overnight.

1845   Accepts co-editorship of the *Broadway
       Journal*. Publishes *Tales* and *The Raven and
       Other Poems*. Takes over *Broadway Jour-
       nal*, which fails.

1846   Writes "The Cask of Amontillado." Moves to
       Fordham where he and Virginia are very ill.
       Writes "Ulalume."

1847   Virginia dies on January 30.

1848   *Eureka* is published. Lectures in Lowell,
       and Providence. Engaged briefly to the
       widow Helen Power Whitman.

1849   Writes "For Annie" and "Annabel Lee." Be-
        comes "engaged" again to the now-widowed
        Sarah Royster Shelton, his first sweetheart.
        Dies on October 7 in Baltimore.

1

Introduction

> To the few who love me and whom I love—to those who feel rather than to those who think—to the dreamers and those who put faith in dreams as in the only realities. . . .
>
> Edgar Allan Poe, *Eureka*

Edgar Allan Poe was in many ways a man of our own time. His poems, tales, and essays transport the reader on fantastic journeys into idyllic and terrifying spheres, where a mummy embalmed for thousands of years suddenly comes to life and where the dead converse with the living and with each other. Such subjects as revivification, hypnotism, extrasensory perception, déjà vu, and psychokinesis (the power of the mind to move a physical object without the aid of mechanical means) are explored, as well as the significance and relationship of God and matter.

According to such authorities as Jules Verne and H. G. Wells, Poe was the first to write modern science fiction; his range extended from interstellar balloon travel to encounters with vast oceanic depths replete with gigantic waves and sucking maelstroms. He also was the inventor of the detective story; his tales of ratiocination, as they are called, feature the master detective C. Auguste Dupin, who, through his use of deductive reasoning, inspired the great Sherlock Holmes.

Poe was likewise a man of our time in his con-
centration on the human psyche; his explorations
into the rational and irrational worlds are fascinating
and fearsome. Much of those writings may be seen
as probings into his own inner world, the gropings
of a solitary, alienated man in a society that neither
understood nor valued his unusual literary talents.
Orphaned before he reached the age of three, deprived of the love and security so necessary to a
child's emotional well-being and development, he
became a tortured, lonely, divided introvert, living,
symbolically speaking, enchained in the dungeon
cell of his subliminal sphere. Poe knew only too well
the utter desolation and isolation of the gifted man
of superior ability living in an almost exclusively
mercantile society.

Poe, however, was also a man of his time. Influenced by eighteenth- and nineteenth-century
scientific and rational views, he was conversant with
the writings of Newton, Laplace, Herschel, and
Humboldt. The English romantic school—Coleridge, Byron, Keats, Shelley, De Quincey—also had
an enormous impact on his creative work, inspiring
him and eliciting from him moments of rapture and
lacerating pain. The works of Schelling and Schlegel, Schopenhauer, Tieck, and E. T. A. Hoffmann
were instrumental in inspiring many of Poe's tales,
particularly in the creation of his heroines: Berenice,
Ligeia, and Morella. The emergence of the Gothic
novel, as practiced by Horace Walpole, Monk Lewis,
and their American counterparts Charles Brockden
Brown and Edgar Huntly, was vital in fostering Poe's
natural penchant for the macabre, the violent, and
the supernatural—his descriptions, for example, of
gloomy and labyrinthine medieval castles with their
trap doors, dungeons, and secret hiding places that

send chills up and down the spine of even the most sophisticated reader.

As a poet, Poe will live as long as the English language. His lyrics possess magic; his poems are songs; they are pure melody. Like a mantra, their power infiltrates body and soul, vibrates and pulsates in keeping with universal rhythms. For this reason I have not attempted to explicate his poems metrically or linguistically. To do so might mar for the reader the beauty of their unique verbal and visual sonority. Such poems as "Tamerlane," "Al Aaraaf," "Israfel," "The Raven," "Lenore," "Ulalume," and "Annabel Lee" are haunting poignant blendings of mind and heart, mosaics of harmonies and color tones. They should be read aloud, allowing the emotional feeling and words to suffuse the atmosphere, to permeate and stir the senses and imagination, awakening the reader to new encounters and fresh experiences.

Poe's tales take place both within and without the rational objective world. They lure the reader into what Charles Baudelaire termed the "secret chambers of the mind." I have attempted to explicate some of these tales from a philosophical, mystical, and psychological standpoint, dividing them into four groups, each exploring a separate dimension of Poe's creative oeuvre: descent, anima, shadow, and mystical quest.

Poe's sea tales—"MS. Found in a Bottle" and "A Descent into the Maelstrom"—expose the reader to apocalyptic visions of shipwreck and destruction, where gaping maws terrify as they open to grab, suck down, and destroy their prey. Such outbreaks of nature with their incredible swirling, whirling forces cause death and destruction, but viewed symbolically, this very force and turbulence may bring about a reorientation of values and a rebirth into a better world.

Poe's anima figures, his feminine characters—Berenice, Ligeia, Morella, Madeline Usher, and others—are not lustful, sensuous, or even flesh-and-blood women. They are Platonic essences; disembodied, unworldly, spectral shadows, they roam or float about their dark habitats. Other subtle vampire types are also present in these tales, destroying the unsuspecting passive male narrators in the most insidious of ways.

Poe's shadow figures, his negative or destructive masculine creations, are for the most part pathological beings who project their hostility, rage, hatred, and murderous instincts in the most rational and highly objective way. Poe's investigations into the world of the psychopathic are clear, concise, and scientifically ordered, revealing the rationale behind each criminal act and the pathology of the disturbance in question, but always after the fact. His narrators are for the most part completely passive. Accepting unquestioningly their predicament and agonies, they never really try to alter their lot.

The final section, "The Mystical Quest," includes those tales and writings which take the reader into unknown realms. Deeply influenced by Plato and by the pre-Socratic and Neoplatonic philosophers, by such metaphysicians as Boehme and Swedenborg, and by such medical men and scientists as Gall, Mesmer, and Laplace, Poe discloses his thoughts on matter and on the One or Universal Soul in such works as "The Colloquy of Monos and Una," and "The Power of Words." There is a parapsychological dimension present in "Metzengerstein," "Mesmeric Revelation," "The Facts in the Case of M. Valdemar," and "Some Words with a Mummy," representing Poe's searchings into what today we call hypnosis, mental telepathy, synchronicity (meaningful coincidences), and psychokinesis. Dreams are described—prodromal (forewarning of a disease) and premonitory—as are beatific ones. Each tale kindles terror and proves fascinating in its own right, exposing the subtle forces at work, the never before experienced, the untried and unforeseen.

Poe's great influence on the French symbolist poets was largely due to Charles Baudelaire, who translated most of Poe's works into French. At a time when the United States and England either denigrated or ignored Poe's work, Baudelaire saluted him as his "mystic brother," so taken was he by the American's theories on beauty, music, intuition, imagination, artifice, and the visionary experience as enunciated in "The Poetic Principle," "The Philosophy of Composition," and "The Letter to B. . ." He responded powerfully to Poe's aristocratic mentality, his aloofness of manner, and his dandy ways. Rimbaud and Verlaine also felt Poe's impact: the music of his verse, his black moods, macabre humor, and the frightening tenor of his imaginings. Mallarmé, who translated some of Poe's poetic works, paid tribute to him in his poem "Tel qu'en Lui-même enfin l'éternité le change"; and his anti-hero, Igitur, who descended the winding stairs of his inner world, was unquestionably modeled after one of Poe's creations. For Valéry, Poe's work was "the act and exigency of an intelligence the like of which is not to be observed to the same degree in any other literary career."

The black, macabre moods and fantastic visions of Poe also affected such decadent writers as Huysmans, Villiers de l'Isle Adam, and D'Annunzio. In fact, Roderick Usher might well have been the prototype for Huysmans's protagonist Des Esseintes, with both men being immured in their own solipsistic domain and both suffering from a frightening, incapacitating neurological disease. Poe's exoticism, his delicacy and elegance, his introversion and narcissism served later as role models for Oscar Wilde and Aubrey Beardsley.

Poe's sardonic humor, his way of distorting reality, his rejection of the pat, the proven and tried, fascinated Alfred Jarry, the father of absurdist theatre. André Breton, the founder of surrealism, was likewise taken with Poe's irony, satire, and tongue-in-cheek verbal assaults and his bent for the macabre, the pathological and the tenebrous. Poe's impact on American and English literature in general was and is vast, affecting such writers as Hawthorne and Melville, Robert Louis Stevenson, Conrad, and Faulkner.

In Jungian terms, Poe was a thinking type who felt most comfortable in the abstract, impersonal, rational sphere. Mentally he was forever exploring, learning, inquiring into the known and the unknown. He read omnivorously: poetry, fiction, scientific and mathematical treatises, mystical and metaphysical tracts. Long before Einstein, he suggested that the "Universe of Stars" was finite and found wanting the axioms of Euclidean geometry, because they failed to answer vital questions about spatial relationships. The universe was for Poe a living organism, a single form that, when manifested, acquired multiplicity. In *Eureka*, his cosmological prose poem, he wrote: "In the original unity of the first thing lies the secondary cause of all things, with the germ of their inevitable annihilation," thus intuiting the big bang theory—the emergence from primordial chaos, nothingness, unparticled matter, from God.

Poe's mind was forever restless, seeking, inquiring, and questioning. Often tormented, never at rest, never serene, it enabled him, however, to realize his own description of happiness. In "The Power of Words" he wrote: "Ah, not in knowledge is happiness, but in the acquisition of knowledge! In forever knowing, we are forever blessed; but to know all were the curse of a fiend."

2

The Life

From childhood's hour I have not been
As others were—I have not seen
As others saw—I could not bring
My passions from a common spring—
From the same source I have not taken
My sorrow—I could not awaken
My heart to joy at the same tone—
And all I lov'd—I lov'd alone—

"Alone" (1829)

"I am a Virginian—at least I call myself one,"[1] Poe wrote, despite the fact that he had been born in Boston on January 19, 1809, the same year that saw the birth of such disparate men as Charles Darwin, Abraham Lincoln, and Alfred Tennyson.

When Poe was two and a half years old, he set eyes on Virginia, when his beautiful and talented young actress mother, Elizabeth Arnold Poe, arrived in Richmond as a member of Placide's acting company, accompanied not only by Edgar but by the newly born Rosalie.

Richmond, then comprising some ten thousand people, was beautiful to look at, particularly when the fruit trees and magnolias were in bloom, with its stately white mansions along the James River, large cotton and tobacco plantations, and rolling hills and fields. Since 1779 the capital of Virginia, it could boast of having played host in the past to such dignitaries as Patrick Henry, Chief Justice John Mar-

shall, and John Randolph, and it received frequent
visits from not only Madison but Jefferson and James
Monroe. Many distinguished men of letters came to
lecture there, including Thomas Moore, the author
of such favorite poems as "Believe Me if All Those
Endearing Young Charms," and Charles Dickens,
about whom Poe was later to write that his characters
in *The Old Curiosity Shop* were "true creations"
and belonged "to the most august regions of the
Ideal."[2]

Placide's company of actors had reached Richmond at the height of the theatrical season, and during the summer months their performances were
well attended. By September, however, when au-
tumn was in the air, their audiences dwindled. Per-
formers were not paid when they did not act, and
Mrs. Poe found herself in a critical situation. Not
only was she virtually destitute, she was also suffering from an advanced case of tuberculosis.

Elizabeth Arnold Poe's life had been far from
easy. She was born in England, but her parents had
destined her for the stage, and they moved with her
to Boston, where opportunities for furthering an acting career were said to be great. At fourteen, Elizabeth was playing Ophelia; at fifteen, she married
a fellow actor, Charles Hopkins; at eighteen, she was
widowed. She toured continuously, playing in cities
from Boston to Charleston, South Carolina. She was
well trained, experienced, and appreciated. When
she met the handsome but untried actor David Poe,
Jr., they fell in love and were married in 1806. Together the couple played in Boston and then traveled
the usual circuit from Boston to Philadelphia, Baltimore, Richmond, and Charleston. Elizabeth's theatrical notices were always excellent; critics recognized her talent and fine training. That David Poe
was less well regarded as an actor may in part ex-

plain the growing tension between husband and
wife. In any event, after their first son, William
Henry, was born in 1807, he was sent to live with
his grandfather Poe's family in Baltimore. David
Poe, Sr., was always called the General, though
he actually had reached only the rank of major in
the Revolutionary Army, but he was a distinguished
man who had provided Lafayette with supplies
and advanced the new government $40,000, for
which he was never reimbursed. The son of John
Poe, a day laborer who had come to America
from northern Ireland prior to the revolution, he
was one of many first-generation Americans who
had made good.

Elizabeth and David Poe continued their stage
careers. She played Cordelia to her husband's Edmund in *King Lear* and continued to act until two
weeks before Edgar's birth, resuming work three
weeks later as Rosamunda in *Abellino the Great
Bandit*. Money was scarce, and David Poe borrowed
from his relatives; acting jobs were becoming even
harder to get. When John Howard Payne joined the
company and took over David's roles, his drinking,
which had already become a problem, increased, as
did his outbursts of temper. To make matters worse,
Elizabeth was already again pregnant when her
husband abandoned her.

When Elizabeth Poe first reached Richmond
with Placide's company, she managed relatively
well; then her salary stopped after business slack-
ened, food grew scarce, and her illness worsened.
She found herself poverty-stricken with two-year-
old Edgar and the baby Rosalie on her hands. For-
tunately, her plight became known, and aid was
swiftly forthcoming. A letter written by the sister of
a plantation owner, Samuel Mordecai, describes the
situation.

A singular fashion prevails here this season—it is charity. Mrs. Poe, who you know is a very handsome woman, happens to be very sick, and ... destitute. The most fashionable place of resort, now is—her chamber—And the skill of cooks and nurses is exerted to produce her delicacies.[3]

Both Mrs. John Allan and Mrs. William MacKenzie showed great kindness to Elizabeth Poe, bringing food and the comforting reassurance that they would care for her two small children should the necessity arise. Elizabeth Poe died on Sunday morning, December 8, 1811. Mrs. Allan brought Edgar home with her to live, and Mrs. MacKenzie took Rosalie, unaware at the time of the fact that the baby girl was slightly retarded.[4]

Frances Keeling Valentine Allan, a tender, understanding, but unassertive woman, was dominated by her strong and ambitious Scottish-born husband, John Allan, who at this time was only moderately well-to-do. In 1800 he had started a merchandising business with a friend, Charles Ellis, buying and selling tobacco, grain, flour, tea, coffee, and other products. The Allans lived over the store of Ellis and Allan, General Merchants, and the child, Edgar, must have felt some comfort at the thought of living in a reasonably stable household, making up perhaps for the feelings of intense insecurity he had known when touring first with his parents and then alone with his mother and sister, and finally, losing his mother through her death. Although there is no substitute for a devoted mother, particularly one as openly affectionate as Elizabeth Arnold Poe, Mrs. Allan was apparently very tender and thoughtful in her care of the little boy. John Allan could be a convivial, outgoing sort of person when the spirit moved him, reciting long passages from Shakespeare and regaling his family with stories of his home in Ay-

shire, Scotland, and tales of sailing ships tossing on
stormy seas.

In 1815, when Poe was six years old, both the
War of 1812—called by some the "second war for
American independence"—and the Napoleonic wars
ended. Commerce with Britain reopened, and for
enterprising merchants like Allan and Ellis, this
seemed to offer excellent possibilities. Allan, it was
decided, would go to London and open a branch
office there. The Allans and Edgar sailed for England that June.

Once in London, Edgar was sent to the Misses
Dubourg's Boarding School on Sloane Street. There
he worked hard and did well. After two years, having
completed the needed requirements, he was enrolled in the Manor School, located in the Stoke
Newington village not far from London. The elm-
shaded street on which the school was located dated
back to Tudor times, as did the high oak-ceilinged
schoolrooms with their Gothic windows and hand-
hewn desks and the tortuous passages and complex
stairs of the school building itself,[5] which Poe years
later reproduced in "William Wilson." Poe, who was
nine at the time, led his class; he read widely, enjoyed his studies, and was already an excellent student in French and Latin.

Allan's business, however, fared less well, and
he and his family returned to Richmond in June
1820, just five years after their departure. Their
homeward journey lasted thirty-six days, and the
frightful storms which they incurred at sea affected
Edgar deeply, since later he would flesh out his
sensations in "MS. Found in a Bottle" and *"The
Narrative of Arthur Gordon Pym."*

Once back in Richmond, the Allans were invited
to share the Ellises' house on the corner of Franklin
and Second streets. The two families lived together

for nearly a year. Business was poor; prices had dropped after the prosperity that had immediately followed the end of the war.

Poe was enrolled at the Joseph H. Clarke School. He wrote quite a bit of verse at this time and must have shown it to Allan, since the latter expressed enthusiasm for the boy's talent. It was at Burke's Academy, to which Poe transferred, that he first began mixing with the Richmond elite, with the Stanard, Selden, and other families. It was here too that he perhaps felt the first twinge of shame at his own heritage. Becoming conscious of the fact that he was the son of impoverished theatrical parents and that his lineage was far from what aristocratic Southern society would approve may account in part for Poe's proud and increasingly lonely and introverted nature. Many years later he was described by his friends as "self-willed" and "capricious." An added factor undoubtedly was that although John Allan was his godfather, he never legally adopted Poe, which meant that his situation was not regularized; nor did Poe receive the comfort of social standing and economic security that he doubtless craved.

Whatever Poe's anger and resentment, however, he kept his feelings well under control. But although he was silent on the subject, an unconscious bitterness may have already made inroads in his personality. He was excessively sensitive lest his schoolmates take advantage of him. They could not intellectually, for he almost always stood at the top of his class. Nevertheless, envy, ire, and contempt all became factors involved in the increasingly complex personality that was Poe's.

He spent long hours alone, reading, writing poetry, and taking walks through the fields and city streets, but he also enjoyed athletics and was a fine swimmer; he is known to have swum six miles against the current across the James River. He took pleasure in the military drills that were part of the curriculum at Burke's Academy and in participating in the celebration to honor General Lafayette during his visit to Richmond in the fall of 1824.[6] He also had at least one friend, Robert Stanard, who admired Poe and often invited him to his home. There Poe became entranced with Mrs. Stanard, a kind and gracious lady who not only listened to Poe's wants but comforted him when his heart was heavy. He felt and responded to the warmth of her personality; he enjoyed being in her elegantly furnished home. He looked up to her and loved her deeply in an ideal spiritual way, and it was to her that he dedicated perhaps one of his most famous and certainly one of his best poems, "To Helen." Her beautiful presence—for Poe she was another mother figure—was to be snatched from him prematurely. She died of a brain tumor on April 28, 1824.

Richmond was a cultural center, and for Poe it served as an intellectual catalyst. A fine museum had opened in 1817. Besides paintings and sculpture, it had collections of fossils and minerals. Such artifacts must have been a treasure trove for the young lad, his imagination thriving on the excitement of seeing the ancient past right before him. In 1823, an Egyptian mummy lent by the city of Thebes was exhibited in Richmond. Perhaps it was this which later provided Poe with the theme for one of his most astounding stories, "Some Words with a Mummy." Lectures on all sorts of subjects, including phrenology, were also given in Richmond. Whether Poe actually attended any of them is not known. Phrenology, however, was much discussed and might have whetted his interest in it and his later emphasis on it in such tales as "The Fall of the House of Usher."[7]

Allan's business was faltering, and he and Ellis finally dissolved their partnership. It was a difficult time in the Allan home. But still more important and painful for Edgar was the discovery of Allan's extramarital relationships and the fact that he had fathered an illegitimate child, the first of several with different women. Poe's manner was always reserved; now a melancholy look became engraved on his face. He no doubt deeply resented the affront to Mrs. Allan; his allegiance to her, the only real mother he had ever known, was complete. Still, he controlled his resentment and maintained his reserve. In a letter Allan wrote to William Henry Poe, he referred to Edgar as showing little affection for him and "not a particle of gratitude" for all "my care and kindliness toward him." This was understandable since Poe was aware of the breach in honor and integrity that Allan, a moralizing Presbyterian, displayed in his behavior.

In 1825, Allan's financial situation improved drastically when his uncle, William Galt, died and left him a great deal of money. The Allans moved into an elegant home in a fine neighborhood at Fifth and Main streets, with a view of the James River. Poe was given special tutoring preparatory to his entering the University of Virginia, founded the previous year by Thomas Jefferson. It was during this period too that he met and became secretly engaged to his first love—Sarah Elmira Royster—who was then sixteen.

Happy with the thought of a requited love, Poe left for Charlottesville and the University of Virginia on the seemingly auspicious date of Saint Valentine's Day, 1826. Like the hero of his confessional poem "Tamerlane," he felt ready to conquer the world.

The University of Virginia is located in a most

beautiful section of the state, near the Blue Ridge Mountains. It is a region studded with fields and forest, with winding wooded trails and crystal-clear streams. To Poe, who was the one hundred and thirty-sixth student listed in the matriculation book of the University of Virginia,[8] the prospect was pleasing and the future bright. Allan, however, although now a wealthy man, began stinting Poe financially. He failed to provide him with sufficient funds with which to live and pay his tuition. Poe could not afford to buy a bed, furniture, clothes, meals, or books. He wrote to Allan immediately concerning his plight but failed to receive a fraction of what he needed. He had to borrow money from the very outset. Although he worked hard and enjoyed his studies, he by no means spent all his time in intellectual pursuits. He took up gambling, hoping in this way to acquire enough money to pay off his debts and needs at the university. It was at this time that he first began to indulge in drinking. According to his contemporaries, his physical make-up or neurological condition could tolerate only a very small amount of alcohol. Even a single glass "was sufficient to rouse his whole nervous nature into a state of strongest excitement, which found vent in a continuous flow of wild, fascinating talk that irresistibly enchanted every listener with siren-like power."[9]

Despite his drinking and his gambling, Poe became a fine French and Latin scholar; he also read in Greek, Spanish, and Italian. He was known for his excellent memory, and he obtained distinction in his final examinations in Latin and French. Nevertheless, his frustrations increased, as did his moodiness. His indebtedness by now had amounted to two thousand dollars, and he could not even afford to buy the necessary firewood with which to warm his room. Certainly the thought of his beloved Sarah must have consoled him in his loneliness. Yet even here he met with disappointment and frustration. Although he wrote many a letter to her, Poe failed to receive a single reply.

Presently Poe was informed that because of his debts, his gambling, and his drinking, at the end of the semester, his "connection with the University was [to be] dissolved." On December 15, 1826,[10] he returned to Richmond in disgrace. To make matters worse, he promptly discovered that his engagement to Sarah Royster had been broken and that she was about to marry another man, A. Barrett Shelton. Years later he found out that his letters to her and hers to him had been intercepted by Sarah's father, who had learned of Allan's antagonism toward Poe. If Poe was not to inherit his foster father's fortune, a better match for his daughter must be found. As for Allan, he looked upon Poe as a wastrel, a reprobate, and a most ungrateful and unsatisfactory young man. Things came to such a pass that Poe, possessing neither money nor training, precipitately left the Allan household. "My determination is at length taken," he wrote Allan on March 19, 1827, "to leave your house and endeavor to find some place in this world, where I will be treated—not as *you* have treated me—."[11] A day later, he again wrote to Allan: "I am in the greatest necessity, not having tasted food since yesterday morning. I have no where to sleep at night, but roam about the Streets—I am nearly exhausted."[12] This was the first but not the last time Poe went without food for lack of funds, and he implored Allan to forward him some money. A few days later, when no answer had come, he requested Allan to send him his trunk and pay for his trip to Boston, where he intended to enlist in the United States Army. Although Allan still failed to reply, Poe did receive a small sum from an unknown source, perhaps Mrs. Allan. He accordingly sailed for Boston on April 3, and after spending seven long weeks of extreme poverty in the city of his birth, he enlisted in the army as a private under the name of Edgar A. Perry. Although Poe's life at this time must have been particularly harrowing, he did meet with one stroke of good fortune. He met a printer, Calvin F. S. Thomas, who agreed to publish a collection of Poe's verses: *Tamerlane and Other Poems*, "By a Bostonian."

Poe, who was of medium height, with gray eyes and dark-brown hair, took to military life, although he found it difficult at first. He did enjoy the fact that he was clothed and fed and that his worries along these lines had been dispelled. He trained and drilled and learned to live with all sorts of people. When his superiors discovered that he not only could read and write but also was a good mathematician, capable of keeping financial records, he was assigned to help in the commissary and from there advanced to company clerk. In November he embarked with his company for Fort Moultrie, on Sullivan's Island in the harbor of Charleston, South Carolina. Poe remained in the South for the rest of his time in the army.

It was a welcome change. He had more leisure time and was able to roam through the countryside, where he had the good fortune to meet Dr. Edmund Ravenel, who was an expert on natural history. They often went on walks together, studying shells and all sorts of marine and plant life. Here too Poe first became fascinated with the many legends concerning pirates and buried treasure, which perhaps inspired "The Gold-Bug." As for his military career, Poe was twice promoted, first in May 1828 and then in January 1829 to the rank of sergeant major.

Poe shortly became dissatisfied with the lot of

the noncommissioned officer. He wanted to spend
more time reading and writing and indulging in a
world of reverie. He also learned that Mrs. Allan
was extremely ill, and he wrote to Allan begging for
a reconciliation and asking Allan to provide him with
a letter which, thanks to the good offices of the colo-
nel of his regiment, would gain him release from
the army. Allan acceded to the reconciliation, but
the letter came too late for Poe to reach Richmond
before the death of Mrs. Allan. He arrived in Richmond the day after her funeral, and his grief was
immense.[13]

Poe decided that his next step should be to en-
roll at West Point, but he needed the proper letters
of recommendation. He gained most of these from
the army officers who had been his superiors during
his stint as an enlisted man in Charleston. The most
important letter and the one of most value, however,
would have to come from Allan. This letter, Poe
learned years later, had been so derogatory that it
may have retarded his acceptance at West Point. In
any event, he waited for months for his appointment.

During this period Poe went to Baltimore to visit
his father's side of the family. He must have been
distressed when he met his grandmother, the widow
of the famous General Poe, now seventy years old,
ill, paralyzed, and living on a meager pension. Poe's
widowed aunt, Maria Clemm, took care of her
mother and her own two children: Henry, age elev-
en, and Virginia, age seven. Money was extremely
scarce, and to add to the household's income Mrs.
Clemm took in sewing. Poe's brother, William Henry, who was dying of tuberculosis, also lived with
them. The poverty and overcrowded conditions
added to the pain that Poe felt when staying with
his relatives, but the warmth and graciousness they
showed him largely made up for the difficult eco-

nomic circumstances. Poe must have been inspired
by the atmosphere, because it was during this period
that he sent a group of new poems, with some he
had already published and revised, to a publisher.
Al Aaraaf, Tamerlane, and Minor Poems was printed
in Baltimore and appeared in December 1829.

Poe was finally admitted to West Point on July
1, 1830. A fine linguist, an excellent mathematician,
and a man well versed in the sciences, he once again
thought that his professional future was virtually assured. Poe studied hard. He enjoyed the work, but
he soon realized that unless an officer had private
means, military life was rigid, meager, and difficult.
Furthermore, he began to doubt that he would inherit Allan's money, particularly now that his foster
father had remarried, and he began easing his
depression and wretchedness with brandy. He kept
writing to Allan, asking him for more money, and
Allan either did not respond or responded in the
negative, finally writing that Poe was not to return
home again. Poe was stunned. He sent a letter begging that Allan write requesting that he be permitted
to resign from West Point. If such a letter were not
received within the next ten days, Poe would act in
such a way as to ensure his dismissal. When Poe not
unexpectedly received no answer, he carried out his
threat. He absented himself from roll call, from guard
duty, and from parade and was finally dishonorably
discharged in January 1831.

Poe left West Point without funds. Ill with a cold
and ear infection, he wrote Allan from New York,
where he planned to live at least temporarily, but
again he received no reply.[14] He also wrote his
brother William Henry, who by this time was a
hopeless alcoholic. Poverty was to hound Poe always, yet in New York he pursued his vision, intent
upon making a name for himself. He again found a

publisher. *Poems* by Edgar A. Poe, Second Edition,
was published in April. This volume, like the earlier
one, contained both new and revised poems—Poe
was always revising his poems throughout his life—
and as a preface, a critical essay on writing, the famous "A Letter to B . . ." Shortly after its appearance,
Poe left for Baltimore and the home of his aunt, Mrs.
Clemm.

Although poor, Poe felt less isolated and rejected now that he lived with the Clemms. He could
communicate with them; they understood his needs
and ideals. He spent much of his time on his writing
and in reading all sorts of works on science, philosophy, and literature. In June he read an announce-
ment in the Philadelphia *Saturday Courier* award-
ing a prize of a hundred dollars to the writer of the
best short story submitted before December 1. Poe
did not win the much-coveted prize, but the five
stories he did submit—*Tales of the Folio Club*—
which included the satiric "The Duke de L'Ome-
lette" and the confessional and parapsychological
"Metzengerstein," were accepted for publication.

Poe continued to write, and the following October when the Baltimore *Saturday Visitor* offered
fifty dollars for the best tale and twenty-five dollars
for the finest poem, Poe submitted "MS. Found in
a Bottle" and "The Coliseum." He won first prize
with the former and was so cheered that he went to
see John H. B. Latrobe, one of the members of the
judging committee, to thank him. A description of
Poe at this time given by Latrobe confirms what
other acquaintances said of the writer, commenting
on his neatness and cleanliness and mentioning that
he was always well groomed, though his clothes may
have been threadbare.

He [Poe] was, if anything, below the middle size, and yet
could not be described as a small man. His figure was

remarkably good, and he carried himself erect and well, as one who had been trained to it. He was dressed in black, and his frock coat was buttoned to the throat, where it met the black stock, then almost universally worn. Not a particle of white was visible. Coat, hat, boots, and gloves had very evidently seen their best days, but so far as mending and brushing go, everything had been done, apparently, to make them presentable. On most men his clothes would have looked shabby and seedy, but there was something about this man that prevented one from criticising his garments. . . . His manner was easy and quiet and although he came to return thanks for what he regarded as deserving them, there was nothing obsequious in what he said or did. . . . The expression of his face was grave, almost sad, except when he was engaged in conversation, when it became animated and changeable. His voice, I remember, was very pleasing in its tone and well modulated, almost rhythmical, and his words were well chosen and unhesitating.[15]

It was at this time too that Poe met another member of the jury, John P. Kennedy, a well-known lawyer and author of *Swallow Barn* and other works who was to prove in the years to come to be one of the kindest of all of Poe's friends.

Poe still longed to clear up his misunderstanding with Allan. When he heard that his foster father was ill, he returned to Richmond. Although the new Mrs. Allan informed him that her husband was too sick to receive anyone, he marched up to the sick man's room. In anger, Allan threatened him with a cane, whereupon Poe withdrew. When Allan died on March 27, 1834, Poe was not mentioned in his will.

Poe was living with the Clemms in Baltimore at this time and continued to do so. After his brother's death, they moved to a small house on Amity Street. Soon Mrs. Clemm's son left for good, and remaining together were her invalid mother, her

daughter, Virginia, now twelve, and Poe. Their relationship was based on love, sensitivity, and mutual
consideration. Poe deeply appreciated Mrs. Clemm's
motherly ways, gentleness, and solicitude on his
behalf. Throughout the rest of his life, Poe was to
call her "Muddy." As for Virginia, whom he ad-
dressed as "Sissy," they were constantly together.

When Poe heard that Thomas W. White, a
printer in Richmond, had founded the *Southern
Literary Messenger* in 1834, he decided that it might
be interesting to become associated with one of the
South's first literary magazines. When he broached
the subject to Kennedy, the older man suggested that
he send White a sampling of his work. Poe did just
that; the strange tale of "Berenice" was put in the
mail. It was accepted for publication, and White
asked Poe to do some book reviews for him. As a
reviewer, Poe was sharp, witty, and acerbic; later
on, when he felt the need, he became devastating
and even cruel.

Meanwhile, his grandmother Poe died, and with
her death, the small pension that had been keeping
the family going ceased. Poe realized that he would
have to contribute to the support of his aunt and
cousin, and to do so he would have to obtain a steady
position. He hinted as much to White, and the offer
of such a position finally came. Poe was made
White's assistant, but he considered himself the editor of the *Southern Literary Messenger*, since he
did almost all the work. His salary was ten dollars
a week.[16]

Poe could support himself, Mrs. Clemm, and
Virginia on ten dollars a week, but there would be
little money left over. He was deeply concerned
when his cousin William Neilson Poe of Augusta,
Georgia, offered to take the mother and daughter
into his home. Poe could not bear the thought, and

he suggested that the Clemms join him in Richmond. He wrote Mrs. Clemm:

I am blinded with tears while writing thi[s] letter—I have no wish to live another hour. . . . I have no desire to live and *will not*. But let my duty be done. I love, *you know I* love Virginia passionately and devotedly. I cannot express in words the fervent devotion I felt toward my dear little cousin—my own darling.[17]

To Virginia, Poe wrote an addendum:

My love, my own sweetest Sissy, my darling little wifey, th[ink] [w]ell before you break the heart of your cousin.[18]

While Poe anxiously waited for an answer from Mrs. Clemm and Virginia, he started drinking and was immediately dismissed by White. He then went to Baltimore, where he took out a marriage license. Mrs. Clemm was agreable to Virginia's marriage to him, but only if White rehired Poe. When Poe promised never to drink again, White gave him back his position. On October 3, Poe returned to Richmond with the Clemms and rented rooms at Mrs. Yarrington's boarding house. Poe secured a second marriage license in good time, and he and Virginia—just thirteen years old—were married on May 16, 1836, the ceremony being performed by the Reverend Amasa Converse, a Presbyterian minister.[19]

Much discussion has centered on the subject of Poe's marriage. Was it ever consummated? Answers vary, and some blame Poe's increased tension and bouts of alcoholism on the fact that he had to—at least for a few years, it is believed—exert extreme sexual control. The truth of the matter in all likelihood will never be known. That he married Virginia, a child at the time, is indicative of his own need for family life and perhaps for a mother figure in particular, a role that the kind and gentle Mrs. Clemm adequately filled. As for Poe's bride, ethereal and tender, she was for Poe the incarnation of his poetic vision. She has been described by others as being very beautiful but in a strangely haunting way. Her raven-black hair, violet eyes, and playfully tender disposition exuded charm, refinement, and sensitivity. Her being was entirely focused on her "Eddy"; no one else counted for her, then or later.

It is unquestionable that Poe was a highly complex, divided man. He rarely maintained long close friendships; he changed jobs frequently, moving from city to city. Misunderstandings also arose with his employers. Psychologically, like Novalis, Hölderlin, Rilke, and so many other romantic writers, Poe can be classified as an eternal adolescent, emotionally stunted, unable to grow to maturity, an adolescent always, moody, perpetually seeking, subject to alcoholism and an overwhelming sense of despair, dependent on others for aid, financial or otherwise. The adolescent also feels at home in airy climes, in evanescent and translucent spheres. In this fetterless world, he can forever escape from the tensions of the outside sphere, but in so doing, he never can achieve independence or balance. He may struggle, try to solve the difficulties inherent in the workaday world, but he lives most happily in the domain of dreams and fantasy.

Poe was indeed an adolescent and his love a very young girl. The thirteen-year-old Virginia looked upon her twenty-seven-year-old cousin and husband as a wonderful father figure—caring, gentle, fun-loving—and Poe tried his best to live up to this image. He also worked hard. He wrote reviews and stories, corrected proof, evaluated manuscripts, and answered correspondence, but he also wrote much criticism upon which he was building a fine reputation, although he also made enemies of those writers who reacted vociferously to his sardonic wit and acidulous attacks. The *Southern Literary Messenger* was gaining in stature and reputation, thanks to Poe. As for the poet and editor, his contemporaries would take note of him in time. James Russell Lowell was to become his friend and confidant, but not Longfellow, whose poetry was one of Poe's *bêtes noires.* Longfellow was a man, Poe said, who wrote "brilliant poems—by accident; that is to say when permitting his genius to get the better of his conventional habit of thinking."[20] Hawthorne, on the other hand, was praised for his *Twice-Told Tales,* which Poe considered the work of a great talent.

Months passed. White, although he admired Poe, felt he had become too powerful and as a result considered his own style "cramped." Poe was not an easy man to deal with. His irritability, perhaps from overwork, may have gotten on White's nerves. Poe's vanity and arrogance—reactions from his lonely and emotionally deprived childhood—often caused difficulty. He could not take criticism, nor did he ever stop asking for assistance—financial mostly—here and there, wherever he could. Certainly he was not a person who functioned well in the world of business, unable as he was to care for even his own material needs. In fact, there seems to have been some element within him that thrived on pain and attracted quarrels, misunderstandings, and trouble.

Poe was discharged from his position in January 1837. He was not overly troubled by the loss of his job, and he felt that White had taken advantage of him. Furthermore, he had gained invaluable experience. Now he could found his own magazine, something he had dreamed about for several years.

He would go to New York City with his family. The *New York Review* had already asked him to send them his work.

Poe found New York crowded and dirty though filled with life and excitement. Moving from the aristocratic South to quarters in Greenwich Village, which Poe thought would shield Virginia from the hustle and bustle of the city proper, was, however, a serious drain financially. In time, Mrs. Clemm took in boarders to supplement the family's meager income. In fact, when the review to which Poe was to submit his articles temporarily suspended publication, she became the family's sole support.

Times were bad. The panic of 1837 was in full force. Poe worked on *The Narrative of Arthur Gordon Pym*. When the review again opened its doors for business, he began writing for it steadily. He also met at this time some fine scholars, including Charles Anthon of Columbia College, for whom he felt an intellectual affinity. He started haunting bookstores in the city, reading all sorts of material and broadening his outlook on many matters. When *Pym* was published in 1838, it failed to win the accolades Poe had expected. In fact, it was criticized severely, and Poe took umbrage. He decided to move himself and his wife and mother-in-law to Philadelphia.

The City of Brotherly Love saw the publication of Poe's metaphysical and parapsychological tale "Ligeia," reminiscent in some ways of his earlier "Berenice" and "Morella," dealing with death and reincarnation—questions with which Poe was obsessed. To supplement his meager finances, he now agreed to revise *A Manual of Conchology* by Thomas Wyatt, a marine biologist. Poe had learned a considerable amount about the subject while in the army. In time, however, this project was to cause him great difficulty in the form of an accusation of plagiarism, but for the moment his literary reputation was not only intact but growing. Some of his finest works now appeared in print: "The Fall of the House of Usher," "The Haunted Palace," "William Wilson." He also began working as editor on *Burton's Gentleman's Magazine* at a salary of ten dollars a week. However, when Burton suggested that Poe temper some of his critical literary reviews and make them less vitriolic and acidulous, Poe took umbrage and severed his relations with Burton and the magazine. After the first glow of anger had subsided, he realized how dire were his straits; when Burton asked him to return, he agreed.

The year 1840 saw the publication by Lea and Blanchard of what was to prove a classic, the two-volume edition of Poe's collected stories, *Tales of the Grotesque and Arabesque*. Fine reviews followed. Still dissatisfied with his own position at *Burton's*, Poe was intent on founding a magazine of his own to be called *Penn Magazine*. He severed relations with *Burton's* in June 1840 and to earn extra funds began contributing articles to *Alexander's Weekly Messenger*, where he started a rage for cryptograms and puzzles on all sorts of novel subjects. These became very popular but consumed much of his time.

It was at this point that he created perhaps his most celebrated character, the detective C. Auguste Dupin, the solver of crime after crime using only deductive logic. "The Murders in the Rue Morgue," "The Mystery of Marie Rogêt," and "The Purloined Letter" will not be explicated in this volume. To do so would be to disclose the secret manipulations, the step-by-step encounters, the ingenious and cunning thinking processes of Poe's great detective and in so doing spoil for the reader the suspense inherent

in the tales. These works should be read and enjoyed
for their spine-chilling effect, the terror and elec-
trifying qualities they inspire. Suffice it to say that
Poe's master detective is a transcendental hero, the
first of a long line of scientifically endowed, creative,
and imaginative solvers of crime. Certainly, the precursor of Sherlock Holmes, Dupin proceeded logically always, as does a calculating machine, yet he
was not an automaton but a clue-hunter, fitting each
segment of the puzzle together so as to create an
impregnable case. Dupin projected himself into the
crimes before him, imaginatively, sensitively, and
always analytically. In "The Murders in the Rue
Morgue," Poe explains Dupin's attitude toward his
work in what might well be a replica of the writer's
own:

[T]he analyst throws himself into the spirit of his oppo-
nent, identifies himself therewith. . . . It is a question of
imagination and artistry. . . . The analytical power should
not be confounded with simple ingenuity; for while the
analyst is necessarily ingenious, the ingenious man is often
remarkably incapable of analysis. Between ingenuity and
the analytic ability there exists a difference far greater,
indeed, than that between the fancy and the imagination,
but of a character very strictly analogous. It will be found
in fact, that the ingenious are always fanciful, and the *truly*
imaginative never otherwise than analytical.[21]

Poe found himself unable to raise the money
needed to start his own magazine. When George
Graham, a former assistant editor of the *Saturday
Evening Post*, became the publisher of *Graham's
Magazine* and offered Poe the editorship, he grace-
fully accepted. Graham also promised that he would
help Poe in time to found his own magazine, but he
never did so. Thanks, at least in part to Poe's editorial skills and the long hours he devoted to his
work, the circulation of *Graham's Magazine* in-

creased from five thousand to twenty-five thousand by 1841.

Poe was finally out of debt; all was well at home. On occasional evenings Poe, who played the flute, would join Virginia as she sang and accompanied herself on the harp. Then suddenly tragedy struck. Although Poe and Mrs. Clemm had known for some years that Virginia suffered from tuberculosis, it was in January 1842, while singing, that she ruptured a blood vessel and began to hemorrhage. For weeks she hovered between life and death. Only through the greatest care and devotion was her life saved. Poe refused to listen to the prognostications of the doctors called to examine her. All he knew was that she must live.[22]

From this time on, Poe's life went downhill. His extreme fear of Virginia's having another hemorrhage—and there were others—more and more fueled his need for the palliative of alcohol, perhaps supplemented by laudanum, as some critics contend. Alcohol buoyed up his spirits and kindled his energies so that he could work long hours, his mind and imagination aflame. Only in this way could he keep up the grueling editorial work and do his own writing and give lectures and readings. He had a particular talent for readings. His voice was warm and melodious and full of deep feelings, and it attracted and held the attention of his audience. Poe analyzed his own emotional plight in a letter to George W. Eveleth, a medical student, whom he met in 1847 after the death of Virginia.

Six years ago, my wife, whom I loved as no man ever loved before, ruptured a blood-vessel in singing. Her life was despaired of. I took leave of her forever and underwent all the agonies of her death. She recovered partially and I again hoped. At the end of a year the vessel broke again— I went through precisely the same scene. Again in about

a year afterward. Then again—again—again and even once
again at varying intervals. Each time I felt the agonies of
her death—and at each accession of the disorder I loved
her more dearly and clung to her life with more desperate
pertinacity. But I am constitutionally sensitive—nervous
in a very unusual degree. I became insane, with long intervals of horrible sanity. During these fits of absolute unconsciousness I drank, God only knows how often or how
much. As a matter of course, my enemies referred the insanity to the drink rather than the drink to the insanity.[23]

Work was a panacea for Poe, an outlet for his
frustrations, his fears, and his anguish. Tales came
in swift succession now: "The Gold-Bug," which
won a prize of a hundred dollars from the Philadelphia *Dollar Newspaper;* "The Pit and the Pendulum," "The Tell-Tale Heart," "The Black Cat."

New York City looked more attractive to Poe at
this point, at least in terms of his career, and perhaps
a new environment would be beneficial to Virginia.
Poe and Virginia decided to find a suitable place to
live, and then Mrs. Clemm would join them. In a
letter to "Muddy," Poe described the quarters they
had found in a brownstone lodging house down-
town. For supper, he wrote, "we had the nicest tea
you ever drank, strong and hot—wheat bread and
rye bread—cheese—tea-cakes (elegant) a great dish
(2 dishes) of elegant ham, and 2 of cold veal, piled
up like a mountain and large slices—3 dishes of
cakes, and every thing in the greatest profusion. No
fear of starving here."[24]

Poe was enthusiastic about living in New York,
as he always was at the start of some new venture.
He was certain that good fortune would be his, particularly inasmuch as he swiftly sold his latest story,"The Balloon Hoax," to the New York *Sun.* He
was right; the story created a sensation; it was followed by the publication of "The Premature Burial"

and "The Oblong Box." But whenever life seemed to smile gently down on Poe and his little family, grief and ill fortune somehow manifested themselves. Virginia's coughing spells grew worse. Country air, Poe felt, was now in order. In his metaphysical fantasy "The Colloquy of Monos and Una" (1841), he had already made his thoughts concerning modern metropolitan life clear:

Meantime huge smoking cities arose, innumerable. Green leaves shrank before the hot breath of furnaces. The fair face of nature was deformed as with the ravages of some loathsome disease (p. 286–29).

Poe took long walks. On one occasion he happened to be walking up Bloomingdale Road—now Eighty-fourth Street and Broadway—and saw a charming 186-acre farm belonging to Patrick Brennan and his family. When he inquired if he, his wife, and his mother-in-law could move in, the Brennans were agreeable to the idea, and the Poes stayed there for some months. Virginia rested, and her husband wrote tales, poems, critical works, and brief statements on various topics—literary, mystical, scientific—which were published in the *Democratic Review* under the title *Marginalia*. Yet, as Poe wrote to his friend, the writer James Russell Lowell: "I am excessively slothful, and wonderfully industrious—by fits." Poe loved to dream, to indulge in reverie, to while away hours, days, and months. During such periods, he confessed, "any kind of mental exercise is torture, and when nothing yields me pleasure but solitary communion with the 'mountains and the woods'—the 'altars of Byron.'"[25]

The year 1845 is perhaps the most memorable for Poe enthusiasts, for it saw the publication of both his *Tales* and his most often quoted poem, "The Raven," a work which has haunted readers young

and old ever since its creation. Poe became famous
overnight. He did not, however, become financially
solvent. "The Raven" brought him the incredible
amount of either five or ten dollars—the sum has
never been officially recorded. Although Poe's writings were being read the world over, selling well
in England and being translated into French by
Charles Baudelaire, the copyright laws were such
that he realized little if any money from his works.

In February 1845 Poe accepted the coeditorship
of the *Broadway Journal*. He would use it, he
thought, not only to recoup his finances but as a
sounding board. He attacked Longfellow at this time
in the most acerbic way, accusing him of plagiarism
and didacticism. He also undertook writing dramatic
criticism, and he gave lectures to often packed but
sometimes empty houses, all of which began further
to sap his vitality and increase his discouragement.
His constant dream professionally was to have his
own magazine, and every time he tried to acquire
the funds necessary, he failed. Miserably ill and de-
pressed, he moved with his little family to the little
Dutch cottage in Fordham, which has been described as follows:

The building is a small one containing only three rooms,
a porch extending along its entire front, and standing with
its gable end to the street . . . the cottage was pleasantly
situated on a little elevation in a large open space, with
cherry-trees about it. . . .

The halfway entrance leads directly to the main room
of the house,—a good-sized, cheerful apartment with four
windows, two opening on the porch. Between these stood
the poet's table, at which much of his reading and editorial
work was done.[26]

Poe worked assiduously on "The Cask of
Amontillado" and "The Philosophy of Composition." Extreme fatigue overcame him; he com-

plained of feeling ill, but only later was it discovered
that he was probably suffering from an irregular
heartbeat. As for Virginia, she was clearly waning.
She was described as looking very young: "She had
large black eyes, and a pearly whiteness of com-
plexion which was a perfect pallor. Her pale face,
her brilliant eyes, and her raven hair gave her an
unearthly look. One felt that she was almost a dissolved spirit, and when she coughed it was made
certain that she was rapidly passing away."[27]

Poe's works were being read in Europe and
America, but no money was coming into the household. Friends and admirers, however, donated bed
linens, clothes, and money for food. The poet wrote
his letters of thanks. Virginia, who had been wrap-
ping herself "in her husband's great-coat, with a
large tortoise-shell cat in her bosom" until blankets
and sheets were given, was indeed grateful. The
chills and fever of the consumptive were increasing;
the house during that particularly cold winter was
insufficiently heated, making matters even worse.
Poe held her icy hand almost continuously, while
her mother clasped her chilled feet, each warming
her as best they could.[28] Mrs. Marie Louise Shew,
the future Mrs. Houghton and the daughter of a
physician, had tended both Virginia and Poe during
the last days of Virginia's illness. She wrote in her
diary that Poe had a lesion on one side of his brain,
which accounted for his bouts of "insanity" when
he took alcohol or drugs; nor did his years of anxiety
and malnutrition and excessive work help the situation.

I did not feel much hope that he could be raised up from
brain fever brought on by extreme suffering of mind and
body—actual want and hunger, and cold having been
borne by this heroic husband in order to supply food,
medicine, and comforts to his dying wife—until exhaustion

and lifelessness were so near at every reaction of the fever, that even sedatives had to be administered with extreme caution.[29]

Finally Virginia died on January 30, 1847. She was buried in the graveyard of the Dutch Reformed Church in Fordham. Poe seemingly could not get on without Virginia. He wept constantly and deeply, wandering off to her tomb, where he remained disconsolate for hours. Mrs. Clemm tended to the chores and wrote the letters to friends and publishers, hoping to place some of Poe's stories and poems in order to earn some money for them both.

It was not long before various women began making overtures, attracted to the striking-looking widower who was always dressed in black and bore so grave and melancholy a manner. During the course of his lectures, Poe had come to know Mrs. Sarah Helen Whitman of Providence, Rhode Island, a widow and poetess.[30] She sent Poe a valentine, and he sent her some verses. She invited Poe to visit her in Rhode Island. Things developed from there, and they were to marry, although they did not. Poe, who had become so erratic, so given to alcohol and perhaps to drugs, meantime fancied himself in love with a Mrs. Nancy Richmond, also of New England. It was she whom he called his "beloved Annie" in his letters. But Mrs. Richmond had a husband, and because she refused to marry Poe, he felt so desperate that he took an ounce of laudanum in a suicide attempt which only made him desperately ill. Still he continued to write to Mrs. Richmond. His letters were filled with rapture and love, "which," he wrote, "burns in my very soul for *you*—so pure—so unworldly—a love which would make *all* sacrifices for your sake."[31]

There was also Mrs. Estelle Anna Lewis, who

lived in Brooklyn and gave him financial gratuities
in return for favorable criticisms of her own verses.
He was so desperately in need of money that he
yielded to her demands.

Despite Poe's plight, his loneliness, and the
complicating women in his life, he still had great
hopes of founding a magazine, relying on his friends
for financial aid. He continued to give lectures,
traveling to Lowell, Boston, Providence, and back
again to New York. He was described as "inspired"
during his readings. "His eyes seemed to glow like
those of his own 'Raven,'" and whether he spoke to
a full or empty house, he held his audience firmly
in his grasp.[32] "Ulalume," a deeply moving poem
about a new love, was written and published at this
time. It is resplendent in the musicality of its lines
but also replete with feelings of guilt, gloom, and
aching pain. Had he perhaps offended his beautiful
vision of loveliness—his great love, Virginia—by
courting another woman? "The Bells," with all of
its tintinnabulating and melodiousness, and "Annabel Lee," with its wistful haunting melancholy,
were also published, as were a number of essays
including "The Poetic Principle" in which Poe
etched his thoughts concerning creativity in general.
Eureka, perhaps his most complex and lengthy prose
poem, was completed in 1848. A fascinating study
delving into the origins of the creation of the universe, its purpose, and its perpetuation, the evolution of souls and Poe's concept of God as "unparticled matter." Dedicated to Alexander von
Humboldt, the German explorer, scientist, and natural philosopher well known for his systematic observations, *Eureka* became Poe's sounding board for
his metaphysical ideas and for his views concerning
Newton's, Kepler's, and Laplace's concepts. Poe's
insights into a perpetually evolving and devolving

finite "Universe of Stars" as well as his views into
matter, which he believed existed only as "Attraction
and Repulsion," are looked upon today by scientists
as incredibly prescient. Poe did not believe in matter
only in energy; his main consideration was what he
termed "the complete mutuality . . . that absolute
reciprocity of *adaptation*" which implies that "each
law of nature depends on all the other laws."[33]

Poe kept himself busy lecturing, editing, writing
criticism, and traveling from Lowell to Boston, to
Providence and Philadelphia to solicit funds for the
literary magazine he still hoped to found. He was
always unsuccessful. On June 29, 1849, he left for
Philadelphia, thence on to Richmond and, he hoped,
a dream fulfilled. When Mrs. Clemm received no
news of him, she grew anxious. He had always written each time he left. Finally, on July 7, a letter
reached her. Poe complained of "spasms" of the
stomach, which he said were just like cholera. They
were so severe that it was impossible for him to hold
a pen. He asked her to come to him, to care for him.

The joy of seeing you will almost compensate for our sorrows. We can but die together. It is no use to reason with
me now; I must die. I have no desire to live since I have
done "Eureka." I could accomplish nothing more. . . . You
have been all to me, darling, ever beloved mother, and
dearest, truest friend.[34]

But Mrs. Clemm never came, not having received the letter in question at that time. According
to extant documents in Philadelphia, Poe, looking
extremely wasted and pale, went to see John Sartain,
the owner of *Sartain's Magazine*, who had shown
him great kindness during moments of need in the
past. Poe asked his friend to protect him against
conspirators—assassins who wanted to kill him and
who were pursuing him. Paranoia had taken pos-

session of him. He begged Sartain for a razor so that
he could shave off his moustache; his pursuers
would then not recognize him. Sartain took him to
his own home, cut and trimmed his moustache a
bit—never giving him the dangerous instrument—
and explained that Poe's appearance had sufficiently
changed so that he would be unrecognizable to his
enemies. He persuaded Poe to lie down for a bit,
and when Poe later insisted on going out, Sartain
accompanied him, fearing the worst. They took a
horse-drawn omnibus and then walked about. Poe
talked incessantly, hallucinating, seeing a blessed
feminine presence before him, speaking to him from
a great distance. They returned home, and Poe finally slept. Since Virginia's death, it seemed that he
had always needed someone with him if he were to
sleep. Alone, his thoughts were horrible and frightening; he was terrified of the dark.

The following day Poe, who seemed to have recovered, left Sartain's home and traveled to Baltimore and then to Richmond. There he gave some
lectures, and he gave more in Norfolk. In both places
he was lionized by the feminine members of his audience, who were fascinated by his strange, enigmatic, and elusive ways, his dress, always black, and
his extreme poise and aloofness. In Richmond, Poe
was befriended by his first love, Sarah Elmira Royster Shelton, whom he again courted and whom he
hoped to marry. He also saw Robert Stanard, whose
mother he had adored when he was a youth.

Life seemed to be taking a turn for the better.
Poe's health, however, was declining precipitously.
Increasingly, paranoia set in. More continuously
now, he felt he was being pursued. His pallor increased, and his voice took on an even more funereal
quality. Fever took hold of him, but despite Mrs.
Shelton's remonstrances, Poe left Richmond for

Baltimore. For six days no one knew his where-
abouts. He was found unconscious on a street in
Baltimore.

There are several accounts as to what followed,
most of which are considered unreliable. His malady
was diagnosed as alcoholism, delirium tremens, drug
addiction, tumor of the brain, and diabetes. The
statement made by the attending physician, John J.
Moran, in charge of the Washington College Hospital in Baltimore where the unconscious Poe was
taken, is perhaps the one authoritative and credible
piece of evidence. It was written in the form of a
letter to Mrs. Clemm.

He remained in this condition from five o'clock in the
afternoon—the hour of his admission—until three next
morning. This was on the 3rd October.

To this state succeeded tremor of the limbs, and at
first a busy but not violent or active delirium—constant
talking—and a vacant converse with spectral and imaginary objects on the walls. His face was pale and his whole
person drenched in perspiration. We were unable to in-
duce tranquility before the second day after his admission.

Having left orders with the nurses to that effect, I was
summoned to his bedside so soon as consciousness su-
pervened, and questioned him in reference to his family,
place of residence, relatives, etc. But his answers were
incoherent and unsatisfactory. He told me, however, he
had a wife in Richmond (which I have since learned was
not the fact), that he did not know when he left that city,
or what had become of his trunk of clothing. Wishing to
rally and sustain his now fast sinking hopes, I told him
that in a few days he would be able to enjoy the society
of his friends here, and I would be most happy to contribute in every possible way to his ease and comfort. At
this he broke out with much energy, and said the best
thing his best friend could do would be to blow out his
brains with a pistol—that when he beheld his degradation,
he was ready to sink into the earth, etc. Shortly after giving
expression to these words, Mr. Poe seemed to doze, and

I left him for a short time. When I returned I found him in a violent delirium, resisting the efforts of two nurses to keep him in bed. This state continued until Saturday evening (he was admitted on Wednesday), when he commenced calling for one "Reynolds," which he did through the night until *three* on Sunday morning. At this time a very decided change began to affect him. Having become enfeebled from exertion, he became quiet, and seemed to rest for a short time; then gently moving his head, he said, *"Lord help my poor soul!"* and expired.

This madam, is as faithful an account as I am able to furnish from the Record of his case.

. . . His remains were visited by some of the first individuals of the city, many of them anxious to have a lock of his hair.[35]

Mrs. Clemm lived on in a church home in Baltimore until February 16, 1871. Rosalie, Poe's sister, who had gone from one institution to another, ended her days at the Epiphany Church Home in Washington, D.C., dying there in 1874.

3

The Poems

> The song springs from an inborn source; anterior
> to a concept, so purely as to reflect, outside, a
> thousand rhythms of images. What genius for
> being a poet. What lightning instinct to simply
> enclose life, virgin, in its synthesis and far
> illuminating everything. The intellectual
> framework of the poem hides—and exists—in the
> space that isolates the strophes in the white of
> paper: significant silence no less beautiful to
> create than the verse.
>
> Stéphane Mallarmé, *Responses to Inquiries.*

"I am young—not yet twenty—*am* a poet—if deep worship of beauty can make me one," Poe wrote. "I would give the world to embody one half the ideas afloat in my imagination."[1] Already he was the author of *Tamerlane and Other Poems* (1827) and *Al Aaraaf, Tamerlane, and Minor Poems* (1829) and the future creator of *Poems* (1831) and *The Raven and Other Poems* (1845), works which Poe was to revise many times in his perpetual search to perfect idea, form, and tonal music.

Poe began writing poetry while still a schoolboy. "O, Tempora! O Mores!" written in 1825, for example, is redolent with the gusto and fervor of youth. Poetry was to remain a passion with him always, a raison d'être, a means of expressing his innermost feelings as well as a way of satisfying his own aesthetic needs. Influenced by such British romantics as Coleridge, Byron, Shelley, Keats, and Thomas Moore, Poe added his own subjective outlook and poetic style, his own very distinctive brand of mystical vision. Nevertheless, as we have already mentioned, he was also in many ways very much a late eighteenth-century man, benefiting from the scientific disciplines of the Enlightenment. Inspiration, he felt, was not enough for any poet who seeks to create a work of lasting value. Discipline and control are a requisite part of the poetic process. A poem must be thought out; it must be sequentially organized, with each emotion and idea logically proceeding from its predecessor, the whole forming an intricate network of unified construction like the Parthenon in its architectural form, remaining indelibly in the memory. Poetry must be shaped, fashioned, and polished like an organic substance. Poe leaned in his aesthetics toward classical concepts that emphasized symmetry, simplicity, and harmony. This was the goal of the Parnassian poets, those practitioners of art for art's sake: Théophile Gautier, Leconte de Lisle, and later in England Walter Pater. They believed that art and aesthetics were in themselves creative acts, one of the goals of life, and suggested that order, discipline, restraint, and craftsmanship were vital factors in all such endeavors. A work of art must be simple, objective, and impersonal so that it may become the common property of all humanity. The French symbolist poets—Baudelaire, who translated so much of Poe into French, and Mallarmé, who dedicated poems and prose works to this "renegade" American—were drawn to him because of the refinement of his verbal feasts and the hermeticism of his thought. Poe both practiced and advocated a poetics devoid of political and moral connotations, based rather on aesthetic considerations, on cool, distanced observations of the subject, using nuanced and glittering tonal modulations.

Intuitive by nature, Poe discovered and explored realms that lie beyond the visible sphere, beyond the dimensions of time and space. In these supernal spheres he experienced an exaltation of the senses that enabled him to penetrate the very heart of mystery. There he probed and questioned, glimpsed visions sparkling with gentle or iridescent luminosity, strange and elusive outlines, shifting opalescent and crystalline light. He perceived both sonorous and inaudible voices, long moments of silences followed by the emergence of outer-worldly harmonies. The writing of poetry excited and tantalized Poe.

It also satisfied an emotional need in him, allowing him to explore the pain of his isolation and loneliness, the feelings of alienation with which his orphaned childhood had left him: "I have many occasional dealings with Adversity—but the want of parental affection has been the heaviest of my trials."[2] Yet in good Parnassian and symbolist tradition, he never directly portrayed his sense of bereavement and affliction in a personal way, expressing his feelings always by means of symbols, analogies, metaphors, and other indirect stylistic means and methods. His inner emotions were encompassed in the mood he created, in the music of the words, the imagery in which he couched his Platonic essences, his visions of ideality and beauty. Poe's verses were depersonalized, filtered through the poetic process, rid of the dross of the outside world, the imperfections that cling to matter. Like the alchemist of old, Poe bathed his images in supernal waters, cleansing and triturating them until they gleamed in inner and outer resplendence, their unvitiated luminosity concentrated in one singularly magnetic unity.

Poe occupies a unique place among the compatriot poets of his time. The older generation of New Englanders were idealists, descendants of the Puritans who had come to build some sort of city of God in the New World. Timothy Dwight, John Trumbull, and John Barlow, in the main, were derivative, imitators of John Dryden and Alexander Pope, Oliver Goldsmith and Samuel Butler. There were also the New Yorkers, Joseph Rodman Drake and his friend Fitz-Greene Halleck, who although fine craftsmen were certainly not men of poetic genius but sophisticated, facile writers about whom Poe wrote a long and fine critique. William Cullen Bryant, an adopted New Yorker, was generally considered the finest American poet in Poe's time. A romantic of sorts, he was perceptive and technically proficient. His "Thanatopsis" (1817), influenced by Thomas Gray and the English graveyard school, was melancholy and austere, perhaps in this regard, not uncomparable to Poe's obsessive interest in death but lacking his poignant imagery and rhythmic musicality. Both the Quaker John Greenleaf Whittier, of the younger New England group, whose interest lay in abolition, and who was a poet of the countryside and nature, as evident in his *Snow-Bound: A Winter Idyll*, and Henry Wadsworth Longfellow, whose *Evangeline* evoked high praise from his contemporaries, were highly lauded at the time. Longfellow, however, was castigated by Poe, who found his writings didactic, moralizing, and devoid of poetic depth and artistry. James Russell Lowell, on the other hand, was highly regarded by Poe, who suggested that his genius was "loftier" than the genius of any other poet of his time. In ac-

tual fact, the work of none of these poets had the
transpersonal qualities and the resonances of Edgar
Allan Poe's.

The concept of ideal beauty was basic to Poe's
ars poetica. Beauty is the core and essence of the
poem, its universality, and its meaning. "I designate
beauty as the province of the poem," he wrote in
his essay "The Philosophy of Composition," published in 1846. "The *tone* of its highest manifestation" is one of "sadness." As beauty evolves in the
written work, it "excites the sensitive soul to tears,"
thereby ushering into the poem a mood of melancholy, a whole emotional dimension. For Poe, melancholy "is the most legitimate of all poetical tones";
soundings of melancholy reverberating around
death, the grief he had known as an orphan and
when he lost his "ideal" love, Mrs. Stanard, his
"mother" figure, Mrs. Allan, and of course, grief over
his wife, Virginia, who was so soon to die.

Of all the melancholy topics, what, according to the Universal understanding of mankind, is the *most* melancholy?
Death which is also the most poetical: "When it most
closely allies itself to beauty; the death, then, of a beautiful
woman" is the most poetical theme.[3]

Although death, implicit in the temporal world,
is equated in Poe's poetic universe with the idea of
metempsychosis (passing of a soul into another body
after death), it also entails change, disruption, chaos,
severing of the ties between loved one and lover,
the agonizing, wrenching separation that rends every
fiber of being: "Death is the painful metamorphosis.
The worm becomes the butterfly—but the butterfly
is still material—of a matter, however, which cannot
be recognized by our rudimental organs."[4]
Such a view as Poe's is timeless; it is Platonic

and Apollonian, not Dionysian, in character. It consists in "the excitement, or pleasurable elevation of the soul," in the delectation of the purest of pleasures life can offer: "the contemplation of the beautiful." Such an appreciation of beauty or of the sense of the beautiful exists "deep within the spirit of man" and is considered by Poe as "an immortal instinct," experienced at its most acute and refined state in the creative artist, the poet.

Poe defines beauty as a transpersonal or archetypal entity that exists over and beyond the chronological, personal, mortal sphere in that fourth dimension of the mystic that no longer bears the impress of the living person grounded in earthly needs. As envisaged by Poe, beauty is divorced from human wants and needs. Like the work of art, it exists in eternal domains.

It is no mere appreciation of the beauty before us—but wild effort to reach the beauty above. Inspired by an ecstatic prescience of the glories beyond the grave, we struggle, by multiform combinations among the things and thoughts of Time, to attain a portion of that loveliness whose very elements, perhaps, appertain to eternity alone.[5]

Supernal beauty can be grasped during instances of ecstatic intuition, when the poet glimpses the pleasures that come with spiritual ascent and his whole being is infused with rapture. During these glimmerings, in some inexplicable way, the unconscious seems to become open to cosmic vibrations; it grasps, mixes, blends, sorts, and rearranges images, feelings, and sounds—conglomerates of infinite particles—into a new awareness.

Intuition for Poe was the great unifying principle that not only nourished but also reoriented the psyche. The poet, Poe suggests in his prose poem

Eureka, must be both a Kepler and a Newton. "Kepler *guessed*—that is to say, he *imagined*" [intuited] the laws of gravitation. Later, Newton proved them logically and reasonably.[6] It is during and after experiencing this very special condition of heightened awareness, Poe argues, that the poet is in a position to acquire direct knowledge. Expressed in mystical terms, the intellect knows, taste feels, and the moral notions oblige.[7] Both rational and intuitive faculties function together. One does not block the other; on the contrary, each flows into and interrelates with the other in a most positive and satisfactory way. The mind therefore functions according to its own laws and logical processes—inductive, deductive, and reductive; taste operates through association of ideas and plays on both imagination and fancy. The great poet, Poe suggested, is endowed with vast intuitive powers, acute intellectual faculties, and a high order of taste. When these function at their best, the apprehension of beauty is possible.

The pleasurable feelings engendered by beauty, as Poe views them, are vastly different from the rapturous passion described by the romantic poets. Passion of an earthly kind, Poe believed, "degrades"; it hampers the poet's ascent to ethereal realms, impedes his visionary moments, distracts him from his obligations, "the contemplation of the Beautiful."[8] Earthly passion undermines the serenity needed for the creation of pure beauty in the poems, the true and real love that is noble and altruistic.

In the search for supernal beauty, the poet must abandon reliance on the logic of overly rational processes, which only bog down the visionary zeal, limit the discovery of extraterrestrial realms, and obstruct the paths leading to unknown heights, those limitless vistas the poet must make his own if his voyage is to extend outside the three-dimensional sphere.

Only in the world beyond the known can the poet experience this pure, giddying enchantment. Paradoxically, once the vision of ethereal essences is grasped firmly in the mind's eye, the poet can return to the mundane world and concretize the vistas opened to him, embedding his new feelings and fresh sensations into multiple rhythms and tonal harmonies. Ideal beauty then can be translated into a language comprehensible to others, with the poet imbuing the symbols and analogies, metaphors, and onomatopeias (words imitating natural sounds) into apocalyptic phantasms.

In each of Poe's poems he sought to express the ideality of his vision; although he realized, as did Coleridge, whom he admired and by whom he was greatly influenced, that the mind is unable to know any realm beyond that of its own understanding or realization. Yet Poe wrote, the poet must endow his work with "the Faculty of Ideality," which "is the sentiment of Poesy." He goes on to state:

This sentiment is the sense of the beautiful, of the sublime, and of the mystical. Thence spring immediately admiration of the fair flowers, the fairer forests, the bright valleys and rivers and the mountains of the Earth—and love of the gleaming stars and other burning glories of heaven—and, mingled up inextricably with this love and this admiration of heaven and of Earth, the unconquerable desire—to *know*. Poesy is the sentiment of Intellectual Happiness here, and the Hope of a higher Intellectual happiness hereafter.

Imagination is its soul.[9]

Ideality for Poe is linked closely to imagination and intuition. It implies a kind of vision that titilates the senses and excites the mind's desire to know, to become a source of ideas, to enhance its power to communicate so that it may apprehend relationships, forms, feelings, and ideas. The road leading to ideality, which calls imagination and intuition into play, is disorganized, a confused mass. To reach such a goal, poetic or otherwise, implies for the mystic the destruction and re-creation of old but worn forms. When, for example, the poet seeks to pierce through the world of matter into a realm beyond, into supernal spheres, he must do away with all earthly, pedestrian, and well-worn paths. Visual and auditory images must take on fresh meanings and tonalities.

The ascension or descent—for the mystic they are the same—of the soul into the Platonic world of ideality allows the poet to appreciate life in both its transpersonal and its personal aspects, resulting in the unification of the universal and the particular. But the fire of inspiration that is known during the moments of poetic creation is not to be sustained, Poe maintained, for long periods of time.[10]

For this reason, a poem must of necessity be brief. One should be able to read it at a "single sitting." If it is longer, intensity flags, interest falters, and the sublime realm is reduced to the paltry and banal. Even such great epics as *Paradise Lost* and the *Iliad*, Poe suggests, are made up of a "succession of brief" poems connected by prose passages.[11] Everything existing in the temporal human sphere is transient and finite, including the creative process. The poet who is unaware that he is destined to fail— in the sense that he cannot know all—is doomed to "sorrow" and to "tears" because his desire will never be assuaged, his imagination being insatiable.

Imagination, Poe maintained, knows no bounds; it energizes the soul's power of ascent and is basic to the poetic process.

The pure Imagination chooses, from either *beauty* or *deformity*, only the most combinable things hitherto uncombined;—the compound as a general rule, partaking in character, of sublimity or beauty, in the ratio of the respective sublimity of the things combined—which are themselves still to be considered as atomic—that is to say, as previous combinations. But as often analogously happens in physical chemistry, so not unfrequently does it occur in this chemistry of the intellect, that the admixture of two elements will result in a something that shall have nothing of the quality of one of them—or even nothing of the qualities of either. The range of the Imagination is therefore, unlimited. Its materials extend throughout the Universe. Even out of deformities it fabricates that *Beauty* which is at once its sole object and its inevitable test.[12]

"Music," Poe wrote, "is the perfection of the soul, or idea, of Poetry" and is an essential factor in the creative process. Music, like poetry, is endowed with meter and rhythm, accented and unaccented beat. Both music and sound are mathematically connected. Poe's understanding of music may be likened to that of Pythagoras, the Greek mathematician and metaphysician.

For Pythagoras and for Poe sounds are based on numbers, with a correspondence existing between them since they are physical phenomena as well as abstract concepts. The harmonies inhabiting the cosmos, which Pythagoras called the music of the spheres, endow numbers with intelligible and sensible plenitude. Both heavenly bodies moving about in our earthly orbit and those in distant galaxies produce sounds, Pythagoras suggested. The musical consonances emanating from the various speeds of these bodies cannot always be heard by the human ear simply because of its physical limitations. They are perceptible, however, to other forms of life—and so is silence. Poe added:

The sentiments deducible from the conception of sweet sound simply are out of reach of analysis—although referable, possibly, in their last result, to that merely math-

ematical recognition of equality which seems to be the
root of all beauty.[13]

Poe frequently used mathematical analogies
when defining his aesthetic and philosophical concepts. "It is *Music,* perhaps, that the soul most nearly
attains the great end for which, when inspired by
the poetic Sentiment, it struggles—the creation of
supernal beauty."[14] The sounds of the harp, which
Virginia played, or the flute, on which Poe enjoyed
practicing, reverberate through increasingly rarefied
matter, and only at certain frequencies can they be
perceived by the human ear. As sonorities rise
through the infinite particles filling the atmosphere,
they are carried through space and light by electromagnetic waves until they reach that "unparticled
matter permeating and impelling, all things" which
Poe defined as God, Unity, One.[15]

When the poet brings forth his work, inculcating
it with beauty and sublimity, he is reflecting God's
design in His created universe. The tonalities of the
words, rhythms, silences, and pauses in the verse
are experienced by nature as a whole, not only by
the human ear but by flowers, grasses, valleys, rivers,
forests, celestial gleamings and forms, each apprehended and mysteriously influenced by the poet's
multiple ideographic exhalations and inhalations.

The poet is visionary and musician, a craftsman
and a master of verbal incantations, a spiritual and
aesthetic guide—a prophet. For the poet, patience
and perseverance are not only necessities but obligations if ideality of the vision is to emerge with
any sort of brilliance and clarity. Although "ecstatic
intuition" and "a species of fine frenzy" are requirements during the stage of initial inspiration,
afterward work must proceed "step by step, to its

completion with the precision and rigid consequences of a mathematical problem."[16]

The poet must work long hours to enforce the
truth of his intuitive images, to express what he
wants "in severity rather than efflorescence of language." A poet must be "cool, calm, unimpassioned,"[17] analytical, in control of idea, logic, grammar, syntax, and form. He must be ever vigilant that
each word, thought, and image be depersonalized
and universalized, divested of those subjective and
personal aspects that particularize, stultify, and
mortalize what must be endowed with the eternal.

A poem should never be didactic or moralize;
it must be simple and precise, an aspiration in all
senses of the word, reminiscent in vision of Shelley's
"Hymn to Intellectual Beauty" and his quest for the
absolute meaning of life. It must be lyrical and pure
in its imaginative course, like the work of Tennyson,
whom Poe considered "the noblest poet that ever
lived." He continued:

> I call him, and *think* him the noblest of poets—*not* because
> the impressions he produces are, at *all* times, the most
> profound—*not* because the poetical excitement which he
> induces is, at *all* times, the most intense—but because it
> *is*, at all times, the most ethereal—in other words, the most
> elevating and the most pure.[18]

Poetry should be lyrical, as Shelley's "If ever
poet sang (as a bird sings)—impulsively—earnestly—with utter abandonment—to himself solely—and
for the mere joy of his own song—that poet [wrote
Poe] was the author of 'The Sensitive Plant.' "[19]
Keats is the "sole British poet who has never erred
in his themes. Beauty is always his aim," Poe
added.[20]

Poetry likewise must not be overburdened with
aesthetic and metaphysical theories; it was this flaw
that did so much to limit Coleridge's poetic élan,

although Poe nevertheless admired him deeply. "Of Coleridge I cannot speak but with reverence. His towering intellect! His gigantic power!" When reading poetry, Poe wrote, "I tremble like one who stands upon a volcano, conscious, from the very darkness bursting from the crater, of the fire and the light that are weltering below."[21] Veracity, not realism, is important. The "willing suspension of disbelief," as Coleridge termed it, must absorb the reader as the poet pours forth his music, having distilled his words, whittled away his emotions, and made manifest his reasoned constructs with their glimmering emanations in keeping with the preestablished design ordered by supernal beauty. Poe's poetry is mystery incarnate.[22]

"Tamerlane" (1827)

"Tamerlane" is confessional in style and high-spirited in its youthful verbal vigor. Poe's concept of his protagonist is Byronic, reminiscent of "Childe Harold's Pilgrimage" and of "Manfred" with its rapturous romantic melancholy and disillusionment, an aftermath of a life devoted to the pursuit of conquest.

The theme of conqueror fascinated Poe, perhaps because his own life even at this early date had been so filled with difficulties and so antithetical to success. When he began writing "Tamerlane," he was about to enter the University of Virginia, and he seemed to look upon himself as a future conqueror in the field of wisdom and a present conqueror in the field of love; he was engaged to Elmira Royster and felt certain of her love for him. Only months later, as we know, when he returned home in disgrace, did he discover that she was to marry another man.

The historical fourteenth-century Tamerlaine, or Timuri Leng (Timur the Lame), claimed descent from Genghis Khan. A fierce and audacious conqueror, he made his capital at Samarkand, having invaded Persia, southern Russia, India, and the Levant and having defeated the Ottoman Turks. Although noted for his cruelties, he also gave encouragement to the arts and sciences and was admired for constructing vast public and architectural works. Possibly Poe had seen Matthew Gregory Lewis's play *Tamerlane*, which was performed in Richmond in 1822, or perhaps it was Christopher Marlowe's *Tamburlaine* that occasioned Poe to write of the Asian despot.

The poem begins as Tamerlane, who is dying, is recounting his life to a priest. In his youth and for most of his life, he had an unquenchable thirst for fame and fortune. "Unearthly pride," he mournfully states, drove him on. His wild ambition compelled him to seek out ever more and more daring and heroic military conquests.

> Aye I did inherit
> That hated portion, with the fame,
> The worldly glory, which has shown
> A demon-light around my throne....[23]

To be victimized by an obsession or ruled by an inner fire is to become, psychologically speaking, enslaved by an archetype—to be dependent for happiness on an unconscious force beyond one's control, to be in the thrall of a primordial or numinous image, making all other values and judgments irrelevant.

Philosophically and metaphysically speaking, the suggestion that Tamerlane was not acting alone, that a driving power determined his fate, "the same heritage hath giv'n / Rome to the Caesar," does not, therefore, hold him personally totally responsible for the cruelties and ruthlessness that governed his life. Fate was the motivating force; it was fate that led him on. Poe's conclusion here parallels the ideas of such mystics as the fourteenth-century German theologian Meister Eckhart, who also believed that he never acted alone but was a representative of God's power, a funnellike force put on earth to carry out the acts of the creator of the world. Like Meister Eckhart, Tamerlane disclaimed accountability for his acts.

Tamerlane had been ambitious and power-hungry—"a proud spirit"—but this not always. He had been born on a mountaintop, with wildness and wilderness as his companions. In time, however, his "brain drank" that "venom" which filled him with an unalterable urge for conquest. Tumult inhabited his soul, chaos his emotions. His feelings mirrored the darkened windswept landscape, the clouds, the erupting light in the heavens, "the pageantry of monarchy!" He listened to the "thunder's echoing roar," reverberating through the peaks and valleys, as if nature itself was arousing his lust for power.

In the stirring verses that follow, Tamerlane identifies his thirst for blood with the earth, and his urge to further his dominions with the heavens. Poe's use of the pathetic fallacy is highly effective here. Nature is personified: hills and dales grow angry; seas swell. In time, however, a more objective view prevails. Tamerlane emerges from the background and realizes how antithetical a force he is, in so doing underscoring his loneliness and isolation.

As Tamerlane increases in years and power, in pride and arrogance, he instinctively looks beyond and ahead of himself—always elsewhere—in an at-

tempt to assuage his desires, neglecting thereby that
important element, the human sphere. (This is the
lot of many dominated by an archetype: the raging
inner fire that forces a person to identify with the
collective and impersonal and not with the individual, the eternal and not the temporal.) "I have no
words, alas! to tell / The loveliness of loving well!"

The past, he now realizes, has vanished, never
to be recaptured. Material wealth fills his coffers,
but as for love, "Its very form hath pass'd me by."
He looks back over his life, recollecting that blissful
time when he "lov'd—and O, how tenderly!" He
envisages the face of his beloved Ada, "worthy of
all love!" as if she were present. As children they
had roamed the mountainside together, tramping
through forests and up crags and swimming in lakes.
Her beauty was pure, her hopes true, her vision un-
sullied. He had always protected her: "My breast
her shield in wintry weather." When with her, "I
saw no heav'n, but in her eyes." She was his guardian angel, his deity. But then the fires of ambition
raged within him, stirring discontent. He left her for
the military life of conquest, pressed on by that
"ambition" which forever set him "adrift."

Now, his days of conquest over, and too late,
Tamerlane realizes all that he has lost. External
triumphs and accomplishments are but hollow fa-
cades; they can never replace a life of real and rich
personal existence. Emptied of harmony, of caring
and gentleness, of love, the feeling principle, Tamerlane's existence is but an empty shell:

> That proud spirit had been broken,
> The proud heart burst in agony.

Unlike Nietzsche's Zarathustra or Shelley's Ozy-
mandias, standing on their mountaintops, Tamerlane
realizes that all he has done has been vainglorious.

His rise to power has only furthered his loneliness; the home which he calls his own is a remote wilderness, frozen and isolated. Love has passed him by; time is irreversible. He longs for his early, ideal love, Ada, but faces instead an empty world, a surrounding void, and a vacant sky.

After he relinquished Ada, Tamerlane saw her once again, but after her death, in that "deep, still slumber," in frozen coldness, never to be warmed again. "A silent gaze was my farewell," he says, knowing that his heart can never know consolation. Her beauty, no longer experienced on a human level, however, continues to grow in dimension and force within him and has now taken on an archetypal power. Transcending mortal contours, she has become for him the "Queen of the Earth." The spiritual embodiment of the feminine principle, she is essence, beauty; over and above, removed from earthly feelings, she stands for love and relatedness in supernal spheres.

A sunless world envelopes Tamerlane. Shrouded in darkness, he now exists as if in a dream, regretting his past and unable to alter his present. Death, so soon to come, is alone undeceiving in these lonely last hours of his earthly existence.

> What was there left for me *now?*—despair—
> A kingdom for a broken-heart.

Youthful passion marks Poe's "Tamerlane": explosive lyricism, rage, and fire. There is also a quality of vague, nebulous feeling, as the mood of melancholy is perhaps most of all prevalent, catalyzing the emotions and weaving a poignant note into the very fabric of the lines. "Tamerlane" is also characterized by what will soon become a Poe constant, a progressive pessimism and despair embodied in stanzas of protracted threnody. In future works also,

however, much of this outpouring of feeling will be
toned down, transmuted into controlled symbols and
lyrical musicality.

"To Science" (1829)

The sonnet "To Science" was written as an intro-
duction to "Al Aaraaf," the title poem of Poe's second
collection. It allowed Poe partially to condemn science for its "peering eyes" which destroy the world
of fantasy, myth, illusion, and poetry; for abrading
"the poet's heart" with its "dull realities," for having
yielded to reason and technological dominion. Poe
was, of course, not averse to pure science: "the
highest order of the imaginative intellect" which is
"preeminently mathematical...."[24] Despite its spirit
of systematization, its colossal preoccupation with
facts and figures, its disciplines encourage the
greatest discoveries—"in the jewelled skies." But
should inspiration run counter to science's ration-
ality, the poet, Poe suggests, will discard the latter
in favor of a flight toward the unforeseen and unheard of. There his imagination will find release
from imitation and bathe in a world of analogies,
pure beauty and sentience, awareness divested of
thought and feelings.[25]

"Al Aaraaf" (1829)

"Al Aaraaf" is a complex poetic and philosophical
work that many critics have analyzed with a variety
of interpretations. Here the rendering is no longer
subjected to tempestuous Byronic emotions as in
"Tamerlane" but transported to the very different

and more restrained music of Milton in *Paradise Lost* and the melodious prose of Thomas Moore's romances, *Lalla Rookh* and *Loves of the Angels.*

According to Muslim theology, Al Aaraaf is the name given to that intermediate realm existing between heaven and hell, the equivalent of the Christian limbo. For Poe, the subject of Al Aaraaf allowed him to explore the relationship of the deity with both angels and mortals, to study such metaphysical events as the Fall and the Day of Judgment. Astronomy, which had always fascinated Poe, also plays a significant role in this poem. In the sixteenth century, the Danish astronomer Tycho Brahe discovered what today we call a nova, but he called a star. He was convinced by its sheer brilliance and strength that it presaged disaster. That same sense of doom and foreboding is implicit in Poe's work.

"Al Aaraaf" also may be looked upon as a kind of *ars poetica:* an exposition of the steps involved in Poe's conception of the creation of a poem, the role played by the imagination in expanding consciousness, by feeling in helping to purify and depersonalize the subjective experience. Poe integrates the Platonic concepts discussed in *Gorgias* and *Phaedo* into his text, revealing the realm of essences and ideas as they exist in the human sphere as well as in the supernatural one.

Part I of "Al Aaraaf" takes place in the ethereal, extraterrestrial plane, in that timeless and spaceless domain where higher intelligences live, beings superior to the human race but inferior to the godhead. Those who inhabit Al Aaraaf are devoid of the powerful gnawing needs and of searing conflicts known to mortals who live in a world of multiplicity and struggle in a grosser atmosphere.

Al Aaraaf lies outside both heaven and the blueness of the terrestrial atmosphere; its opales-

cence exists only for those who obey its laws. This
wandering star, before the poem begins, has already
fulfilled Deity's command, having visited and destroyed the earth and then returned to its astral
heights "near four bright suns." Man, Deity felt, had
to be punished for his insatiable quest for knowledge, the same sin of pride and arrogance that
caused the Fall and the expulsion of Adam and Eve
from the garden of Eden. The thirst for knowledge
by mortals is dangerous since it may overthrow the
cosmic balance and patriarchal domination, leading
eventually to a claim of equality with God and de-
basing the very concept of divinity, of the all, the
absolute. This causes also an identification between
divinity and nature to take place which is equally
an error, for God transcends the pantheistic credo.
He reveals himself to man through His expanding
soul. Punishment was, therefore, in order. The souls
of those who dwelt on earth must atone for the sin
of arrogance.

In Poe's poem "Al Aaraaf," Nesace is God's favorite angel; she is "the idea of Beauty," and as such
she is the ruling presence on Al Aaraaf. A nonan-
thropomorphic entity, God incorporates within
himself all qualities and characteristics, which mortals, living in a finite world—and even inferior spirits
who make their home on Al Aaraaf—look upon from
a limited and therefore relative point of view. Thus,
good and evil inspire fear or awe, love or terror. Even
Nesace, although a superior intelligence in comparison with the others on Al Aaraaf, turns her face
away from the "burning eye" of divinity, unable to
face that blazing force, that totality of absolute light
and darkness which is one, single, and complete.

A shelter from the fervour of His eye;
For the stars trembled at the Deity.
She stirr'd not—breath'd not—for a voice was there

How solemnly pervading the calm air!
A sound of silence on the startled ear
Which dreamy poets name "the music of the sphere."

God's voice resounds throughout the universe, but Nesace alone is able to hear it directly. That God is absolutely inaudible is also known to her through the very notion of silence, a materialization of harmony experienced in mellifluous or strident emanations.

As Poe wrote, Nesace is the epitome of beauty and spirituality, and she is therefore nonmaterial,[26] capable of experiencing synesthesia; that is, she can taste flowers, hear silences, imbibe words, smell rain. The senses, divided in the temporal world, are fused in the rarefied domain she inhabits. Forces and formless entities are endowed with spirit in Al Aaraaf, a nonmimetic realm that opens to its inhabitants unlimited spheres.

Nesace is a presence, a tone, an idea, awaiting God's command. Sometimes in moments of repose, she looks downward and outward to the inferior stars and planets moving about at lower speeds and diminished intensities. Their realms are experienced by her in various hues—purples, golds, opals, whitish whites—not in a single unified color as in the absolute realm of God. Each time she prays to God, the aroma of the flowers carries her voice to him. She begs him to elevate and restore to their pristine purity those lower beings who have come to Al Aaraaf.

Part II takes place in the temple which is Nesace's abode.

Of gorgeous columns on th' unburthen'd air,
Flashing from Parian marble that twin smile
Far down upon the wave that sparkled there,
And nursed the young mountain in its lair.
Of molten stars their pavement, such as fall

Thro' the ebon air, besilvering the pall. . . .
A dome, by linkéd light from heaven let down,
Sat gently on these columns as a crown—
A window of one circular diamond, there,
Look'd out above into the purple air. . . .

It is from these columned halls that Nesace calls out
to those subject to her and brings them together. She
summons Ligeia, the angel of harmony, of the music
of nature, a nonmaterial essence and superior intelligence, to her temple. Nesace commands her to
awaken the spirits of those who lie dormant on Al
Aaraaf. They must assemble and observe the rules
on "the wandering star," devote their time to the
contemplation of beauty, thereby purifying their
natures still further until they too radiate crystalline
clarity and exist in an incorporeal state.

The spirits meet in Nesace's temple. They are
all there, save for the Greek Angelo, who perished
during the catastrophe and who just before his death
experienced the strangest of luminosities, pure light
unbroken into its component colors. In accordance
with Platonic belief, Angelo's soul and spirit then
was allowed to move to a higher sphere after the
earth's destruction. Now, however, looking back in
time and place and seeing his original home, he
seeks to return to it rather than to ascend further.
His beloved Ianthe, who comes from still another
world, believes that the love they feel for each other
is sufficient to occupy their days and nights. These
spirits alone defy Nesace's command. They are so
engrossed in themselves that they do not even hear
her summons. They sleep and love, oblivious to
God's command to devote their lives to pure beauty
and thus to progress to higher spheres. Angelo and
Ianthe hear only their own voices, pursue their own
private vision and reveries, those of inferior beings
solipsistic in nature.

Ianthe, beauty crowded on me then,
And half I wish'd to be again of men."
"My Angelo! and why of them to be?
A brighter dwelling-place is here for thee—
And greener fields than in yon world above,
And woman's loveliness—and passionate love."

Angelo and Ianthe might have soar?d together to purer spheres and enjoyed a spiritualized love in absolute beauty. Instead, they chose the sensate world of passion. In this respect, they are prototypes of Adam and Eve, unworthy in the poet's view of ascending to a higher order. The love they share on Al Aaraaf is of an equivocal kind, visceral, and not of the mind. The godly realm, the mild and peaceful world of perfect knowledge, must forever remain closed to them.

The actuality of God's light will also remain hidden to Nesace and Ligeia. Although they spread God's message throughout the universe in the form of pure idea and supernal beauty, a protective cloud will always surround the mystery of being, the all.

Poe once wrote that he considered allegories "contemptible," but one cannot but look upon "Al Aaraaf" and many other works by him as emblematic of his own metaphysical and aesthetic ideas. Reminiscent of the Platonic quest for the ideal, Poe is concerned in "Al Aaraaf" with spiritual intangibles, with intellectual concepts beyond the scope of terrestrial views, the sphere where truth, beauty, and justice abide. In such a pure ethereal realm, knowledge is communicated through the music of the spheres. If obligations are met and celestial rules obeyed, the contemplation of absolute beauty is the bounty glimpsed by mystics and poets.

Aesthetically, Poe seems to suggest that few poets can experience the revelation of ideal beauty. Its shining beam reaches out to our temporal world from the world of supernal marvels, but not in sufficient strength to make easy the ascension into those higher states, transcending the human condition, where the perfect poem may be realized. The difficulties encountered during the poetic process must, however, be overcome, no matter what impediments are placed in the creative person's path. Conflict will occur and the poet's mettle will be tested each time a new work is begun, for the pure word must be focused upon, rid of dross and weighty matter, forced open to thought, expressed clearly and synesthetically, imbuing it with tone, image, and rhythm, thus revealing a higher order of discipline and imagination, truth, and taste. Music that helps create the poet's structured language aids in the discovery and retention of the truth that exists in a world beyond that of concrete objects, that arcane domain which the poet must apprehend and can once his spirit soars into nonmaterial spheres. In that timeless, spaceless realm where beauty and harmony can further awaken and stimulate the soul's ascension to higher and more radiant domains, the poet may glimpse God, that creative center which is the source of all inner life and light.

As the poet moves into such climes, his sensual passions will be removed like so many barnacles clinging to a ship. He may experience that divine sixth sense once he has cut himself off from human entanglements and pared down his material needs. The Uranian Venus comes into view in "Al Aaraaf," an extended cosmic image comparable to the poet's internal mind and soul. If he falters in his goal, he will become like Angelo and Ianthe, lulled into believing that the outer material world is all in all, an illusion which is the trap that catches all those suffering from hubris and superficiality. The poet of genius, the intuitive seer knows that he must further pursue his vision, refining it into words, rhythms, musical tonalities, and imagistic representations, thus creating a unified construct—the perfect *poem,* a blend of the immortal being and the immortal maker.

"Israfel" (1831)

The name "Israfel" in Islamic legend means the "burning one." This is the angel of resurrection and song who will sound his trumpet on the day of judgment. He is called Azrafel ("help of God") in the Koran.

Poe's poem consists of a dialogue between a mortal poet and Israfel, who lives in rarefied climes, unhampered by human limitations. As in "Al Aaraaf," the atmosphere is vague, phantasmagorical, enveloped in ascensional and descensional imagery, a fitting backdrop for a mortal who seeks a melodious spiritual interchange with an immortal.

"Israfel" has eight stanzas, an interesting number in light of Poe's fascination with mysticism and numerology. According to Pythagoras, the number eight represents two concentric circles, motion pursuing a circular and unlimited round and, in so doing, maintaining cosmic equilibrium. Turned on its side, eight also symbolizes the infinite, thus perpetuating the eternal circularity of all supergalactic and subatomic motion. For the Buddhist and the Celt, the circle symbolizes the wheel of life in its external transformatory rotation.

Israfel, the wise and beautiful angel "whose heart-strings are a lute," knows how to sing the music of absolute poetry, far superior in tone and form to any mortal's creation. He is purified essence, divested of those specific human passions which serve to leaden and deaden the creative instinct, and his musical permutations reduce all beings to silence, so absorbed are they in his tonal reverberations. Like Orpheus with his lyre, he knows how to combine vocal and instrumental sounds in varying melodies, harmonies, rhythms, and timbres, attracting to his orbit the animate and inanimate worlds. All who are exposed to Israfel's melodies dwell in profound thoughts, in spiritual and impassioned sensations as his detached and ethereal emanations spread to the most distant recesses of the cosmos.

> But the Heavens that angel trod
> Where deep thoughts are a duty—
> Where Love is a grown god—
> Where Houri glances are—
> —Stay! turn thine eyes afar!—
> Imbued with all the beauty
> Which we worship in yon star.

Israfel's music provides "fire" and "fervor," and he pours out his ecstatic emotions in purified and depersonalized essences, emotions free of earthly soundings with their multiple grievances, joys, hates, and loves. As his reverberations fill the atmosphere, they captivate feeling, halt sensation, and impose their unity and fullness in glowing, resplendent tones.

Mortal emanations, in contrast, exist in a "world of sweets and sours," a divisive domain where needs are expressed in paltry ways, constricting the poet's vision. Platonic essences are closed to those near the earth. Only in the domain of the stars, far above the routine, can idea merge with number, giving birth to that music of the spheres in which rests the poetic principle. "Music, when combined with a pleasurable idea is poetry," Poe wrote, "music, without the idea, is simply music; the idea, without the music, is prose, from its very definitiveness."[27]

The earthly poet enslaved by imitative forms can particularize his emotions and sensations only by imprinting with his own personal stamp his imagery, metaphors, similes, and other technical devices. He fills feeling with texture and density rather than divesting his verse of these heavier elements. Yet his longing to move beyond the world that surrounds him and leap into untried spheres is there; he seeks to intuit the oneness beyond the world of multiplicity, but he is aware that his efforts are useless, that powerlessness is his when compared to Israfel's heavenly tones.

> Yes, Heaven is thine: but this
> Is a world of sweets and sours:
> Our flowers are merely—flowers,
> And the shadow of thy bliss
> Is the sunshine of ours.

No matter how forcibly the poet longs to exchange his place for that of Israfel, he realizes he must content himself with the mortal world of sensory forces and earthly emotions. "It is but Man's longing for a fundamental First Cause," Poe wrote in *Eureka*, "that impels both his intellect and fancy." Although heaven and earth are separated, the poet's imagination roams free. The poet knows that his poem will never reach the range to which he aspires, yet he does at times experience the headiness and melancholy of powerfully felt moments that he creates.

"To Helen" (1831)

This three-stanza lyrical poem contains lines that have become part of our literary heritage: "To the glory that was Greece, / And the grandeur that was Rome." Written with classical order, "To Helen"

unites beauty and melancholy, two of Poe's favorite
themes, in sequences of images that are a pictorial
feast for the eyes as well as for the other senses. Poe
certainly reached Parnassian perfection in this work,
bringing forth objective and impersonal images of
universal beauty and artistic and technical excel-
lence. James Russell Lowell, poet, editor, and critic,
wrote that "To Helen" was "limpid and serene" and
that its simplicity is reminiscent of "a Greek column
because of its perfection."[28]

"To Helen" has been called one of the most
beautiful love poems in the English language. It was
inspired by Mrs. Stanard, who had been so kind to
Poe during his unhappy teens, consoling him always
with her gentle words and loveliness. In a letter
written to Helen Whitman, Poe stated that the poem
had been "written, in my passionate boyhood, to the
first, purely ideal love of my soul—to the Helen
Stanard [sic] of whom I told you."[29] After her death
in 1824, Poe visited her grave many times, cherish-
ing the feelings of warmth she had conveyed to him
always when he was in need. He may have included
in this poem some of the tender feelings of love that
Mrs. Allan aroused in him when she welcomed him
into her home as her son.

Whatever the inspiration, "To Helen" speaks
for itself as a consummate poetic expression. It
transports the reader back to the days of ancient Ho-
meric Greece, to Helen of Troy, that archetypal image of absolute feminine beauty, a vision born of the
intellect. Although civilizations have come and gone
and loves have waxed and waned, the image of
beauty engraved in the minds of humankind
throughout the centuries has never lost its power
and radiance. The beauty that Helen cast still fills
the universe, flowing "gently, o'er a perfumed sea,"

and although it cost so many lives and caused Odysseus his difficult travels, "the weary, wayward wanderer," it brought rapture, excitement, turmoil, chaos, and finally serenity—all the feelings the creative instinct must know to bring forth such epics as the *Iliad* and the *Odyssey*.

Beauty, like the poem, is the poet's life goal, the highest principle known to humankind, the abstraction, the sublimation of what he experiences in the phenomenological world. The poet, forced to roam on "desperate seas" for long periods of time, concentrates on his goal, on his vision that lives actively in his imagination and ideally in his perceptive eye. He sees Helen with her "hyacinth hair," recalling the young flower god whose beauty had filled Apollo's being with such love and who died early, leaving his impress on the flower named after him, the hyacinth, which even today fills the world with its aromatic flavor, its narcotic aroma arousing the dream and exposing subliminal spheres. Helen's "classic face," symmetrical and regular, in keeping with the poet's tempered objectivity, retains that harmony, that hard and feminine flame, that precision of detail. Her "Naiad airs" underscore the nymphlike aspect of this beauteous woman, eternally retaining her youthful vigor. Time past and time present are fused in one extended poetic image.

Helen's form becomes more remote and less human in the final stanza. Seen in a "brilliant window-niche," she has a "statue-like" stance. The calm serenity of her light and presence will forever remain, and for the poet she will ever be a beneficent presence, a feminine guardian symbol, holding her "agate lamp."

> Lo! in yon brilliant window-niche
> How statue-like I see thee stand,

> The agate lamp within thy hand!
> Ah, Psyche, from the regions which
> Are Holy-Land!

The feminine presence invoked in this last stanza represents the clearest incarnation of Poe's anima, the eternal feminine principle slumbering in his unconscious, distantly shining. No longer Helen of Troy who captivated men by her allure, she has become Psyche—the soul—the inspiration for the youthful poet. It was Psyche who held up the lamp in order to see her lover, Cupid, and in so doing disobeyed divinity's injunction never to view a god. Psyche endured the pain of her punishment and was pardoned; her lover eventually returned to her. Similarly, the poet must experience abrasion and agony in his determination to know supernal spheres and contemplate ideal beauty. But Psyche is also a Christian symbol to the poet, emanating, as he does, from the "Holy-Land." Here the image of the virgin Mary, immaculate in her whiteness and purity, fuses with that of Psyche to create a numinous entity, the archetypal mother who gave birth to a god. It is her beauty, both outer and inner, that gives life to the poetic principle, to the work of art.

"The Sleeper" (1831)

"The Sleeper," originally entitled "Irene," focuses on the most constant and obsessive Poe theme: the death of a beautiful young woman. It is June, a moonlit night; a young girl who has just died is lying on her bed. As the wind blows through the open window, the curtains and the fabric of the canopy move about, casting strange shadows here and there, as if the sleeper herself might awaken momentarily. The beloved dead, Poe implies, must stay close to mortal life on behalf of those who mourn and remember them. Only after there is no longer anyone who longs to hold them here can they find release.

Poe centers his poem on the concept of memory, a favorite theme of romantic poets. In "The Sleeper," the poet-narrator states that death should not elicit merely hopeless mourning and grief. It is in fact a time of transition when the balance between a person's physical and spiritual state alters before being is translated into pure essence. The fact of death does not therefore warrant grief and pain; on the contrary, it should be thought of as a release from the burden of earthly existence and an assumption into a new sphere of being, a penetration and discovery of fresh supernatural realms.

The time is specified in "The Sleeper," and in this respect it is far more definite than the cyclical notions implicit in "Al Aaraaf" and "Israfel."

> At midnight, in the month of June,
> I stand beneath the mystic moon.

Starting from the meridian, in chronological time, the hour of midnight marks the center of the twenty-four-hour cycle, the halfway mark, the first hour of night, preceding the dawn or rebirth of day, a time that played a significant role in the ancient mystery religions, a time when Kabbalists offered special prayers, commemorating a spiritual "catastrophe" on a cosmic level—the hour of change.[30]

"The month of June" similarly divides the twelve-month yearly cycle in half, June being the sixth month, thus underscoring the halved nature of our solar and lunar concepts. (Interestingly enough, the six-month period also could refer to Perse-

phone's stay in the underworld.) Both references to
midnight and to June indicate an isomorphic relationship between number, time, and the psychic
state.

The mystic moon which illuminates the poet's
scenic vision is "an influence dewy, drowsy, dim,"
reinforcing the quiescent mood that the sleeper has
aroused yet endowing it with audible sonorities at
the time by personifying plants and objects: the
"rosemary sleeps," the "lily lolls," as if all nature
were in repose yet actively viewing beauty asleep.

The moon, a favorite symbol of the romantic
poets, receives its light only by reflection, and because of this, it is identified with memory and with
the human psyche. It does not shine with the harsh,
masculine brilliance of the sun but in veiled silver
tonalities, in indirect feminine ways, eerie and mysterious refractions. The poet views the moon in
its triune aspects: celestial, terrestrial, and infernal. Associated with the darkness of the moon is
Hecate, the Greek deity who reigned over the lower
world, tantalized men, aroused ghosts, and haunted
graves. Poe's moon is death-oriented, yet it is neither evil nor terrifying. For Poe, the moon is a
source of despair but also of hope, joy, and madness as it ushers into being a new world born of the
recollected past:

> The lady sleeps! Oh, may her sleep,
> Which is enduring, so be deep!
> Heaven have her in its sacred keep!

An archaic, sepulchral world is evoked at the
conclusion of "The Sleeper"; there his beloved will
rest "remote, alone," there she will continue to live
as his inspiration.

"The City in the Sea" (1831)

As in "The Sleeper," the focus of "The City in the
Sea" is on death. However, its imagery is marked
by constant apocalyptic descents. "Death looks gi-
gantically down," the poet writes, upon mortals and
their constructs, their cities and their credoes that
bind and limit them, enchaining them in an unend-
ing round of life and death.

The city to which Poe refers, although frequently identified with the biblical Sodom and Go-
morrah and sometimes with the legendary lost continents of Atlantis and Lemuria, is almost certainly
imaginary. Powerfully alive in its creator's mind, the
city emerges in all its strange and eerie grandeur, a
necropolis of sorts where once active creative people
lived and functioned, constructing monuments to
eternity.

> Streams up the turrets silently—
> Gleams up the pinnacles far and free
> Up domes—up spires—up kingly halls
> Up fanes—up Babylon-like walls—
> Up shadowy long-forgotten bowers
> Of sculptured ivy and stone flowers—
> Up many and many a marvellous shrine
> Whose wreathéd friezes intertwine
> The viol, the violet, and the vine.

The magnificence of their endeavors and the evocative beauty of their soaring towers and spires and
sculptured friezes have now been submerged beneath the "melancholy waters." For the alchemist-
mystic such an occurrence implies a return to the
original element and therefore to the primal undifferentiated state. The city in Poe's stanzas therefore
may be considered as a symbol of the mother who

cares for and protects all those who dwell within
her domain.

In both the Old Testament and the New Testament, the cities of Jerusalem, Babylon, Tyre, and
Rome are all personified as women and endowed
with various feminine characteristics. But there
comes a time when the mother, no longer fruitful
and forceful, must succumb to her own mortality.
The city thus sinks beneath the sea into the primal
waters that flow in accordance with the universe's
rhythm, and in so doing, all that was "solid" within
its walls is washed away and dissolved, transformed
into liquid, the multiple reverting to the single in
the constant cyclical process in which the component parts of matter return to "the all-embracing
monad," the *quinta essentia*. As far as it is known,
it was the sixth century B.C. Greek philosopher
Thales who first posited that all comes from water.
Homer also refers to the god Okeanos as the "source
of the Gods" and the "source of all things" (*Iliad*,
XIV). In Poe's poem, water is thus the element that
nourishes and protects when future vital life and
growth are possible. Once decadence has impressed
itself, however, disintegration follows, and the de-
composed matter flows slowly back into its original
state—water—to await renewal and restoration until
life again emerges in fresh and fruitful forms.

So the city sunk beneath the sea was in Poe's
stanzas ancient and outworn, its atmosphere stale
and arid. This likewise is the fate of the creative
individual who has reached an impasse in his or her
work, whose desire is only to repeat and refurbish
past themes and phrases, those which are smothered,
lifeless, lacking zest and fervor. When the poet's
worn-out inspiration sinks back into the vast waters
of the sea—or its psychological equivalent, the collective unconscious—that eternal and unlimited

realm which is the source of visions and dreams and from which they, like poetic creativity, are renewed, having been exposed to the treasures that exist inchoate within.

For Poe, therefore, the fate of the sunken city is neither punishment nor reward. The city has left the terrestrial region and gone to an abode buried beneath the moving waters, that is, the ocean of eternity. In this timeless and spaceless realm, like the *aqua permanens* of the mystic, the poet subsumes another world, not the airy climes of celestial regions but the spiritual waters of inner man, the *prima materia,* the potential of all future creations. In this dark region where "no rays from the holy heaven come down," the poet receives strange luminosities emerging from a "lurid sea" in unheard of architectonic forms, archaic and terrifying.

There is no moral, no didacticism or allegory in "The City in the Sea." Death "far down within the dim West" reveals its gaping void, its "wilderness of glass," reflecting the unlimited expanse in a long watery embrace. But like Sisyphus, the poet does not despair. He works and struggles, forever striving to express his inner vision in visual, sonorous, tactile, and olfactory sensations, forever activating and intensifying his feelings as he plunges into the black unknown and sinks deep beneath "a void within the filmy Heaven."

Beneath the ocean of the unconscious, life seems to thrive; plants and fish abound, shedding their colorations under the waves. "A redder glow" indicates the energetic process at work; emerging from beneath the depths, urged on by some exalted force, some transpersonal factor that paves the way for the new and untold. The "redder glow" also may refer to some mystical communion and blood sacrifice that renews and revitalizes all that come into contact with it. The "drinking in the blood" bestows upon the poet renewed life and vigor; it is the bread and wine that feeds his imagination, whets his appetite, and triggers his senses.[31] Spirit and matter are one, as are heights and depths, heaven and hell, good and evil.

Waves now cover what once was visible, obliterate what once had form. The life-giving process is now illuminated by another light, strange and terrifying in its powerful radiations because it conjures forth the unknown, a hell perhaps, but not the evil domain of the Christian, rather the Hades of Pluto, the god of plenty, who offers mortals eternal riches in the underworld. Those who know how to experience them, who struggle to decipher what lies hidden in those porticos beneath the sea or in the poet's subliminal spheres, will be enriched by the experience; they will have perceived the all that exists in a perpetual process of transformation.

> And when, amid no earthly moans,
> Down, down that town shall settle hence,
> Hell, rising from a thousand thrones,
> Shall do it reverence.

"Lenore" (1843)

"Lenore," when first composed in 1831, was entitled "A Paean." Poe afterward revised it several times, and it is the 1843 version that concerns us here. Both dirge and dialogue, the poem focuses on the best way to remember the dead. Should Lenore be mourned, thereby recalling the pain inflicted upon her family and "false friends," or should her death be looked upon as a cause for celebration, marking her entry into a new and happier sphere of being?

The feeling of loss that is caused by the death of Lenore does not inspire grief or acceptance at the outset of the poem:

> And let the burial rite be read—
> The funeral song be sung—
> A dirge for the most lovely dead
> That ever died so young!

The questioner asks the lover, Guy de Vere, why he does not weep when looking at this beautiful form, "rigid" on her bier, never again to inhabit earthly spheres.

The conventional funeral procession, the religious ritual, and the hymns and dirges have all taken place. What do the mourners and Guy de Vere in particular feel? Rather than respond to the question, De Vere alters the direction of the discourse. He accuses Lenore's family and friends of having been cold and unfeeling to this beautiful young creature while she was on earth. They are guilty singly and as a unit.

The reader might expect that Guy de Vere's dirge for "sweet Lenore" would express his longing for his youthful love as forcefully as he focuses his anger on those selfish, unthinking people who once knew her. But De Vere cannot follow traditional ways, which hamper his feeling, his love for Lenore: "No dirge will I upraise." To do so would be to block the feeling contained in the imaginative force of her presence in his mind's eye both then and now. Her flight to angelic spheres should be helped by friendly winds. No mourning bell should toll for his beloved; only an Apollonian song of triumph will he sound as "her sweet soul" is wafted gently up far above the earth, which for her was largely a place of tears during her mortal existence. "To friends above" she ascends, leaving her "friends below" to

their "grief and moan." Henceforth, she will live in
painless realms where she will abide as a soul in
the purest of estates "beside the King of Heaven!"

"The Raven" (1845)

Poe dedicated "The Raven" to Elizabeth Barrett
Browning, "the noblest of her sex." It was alluded
to by Margaret Fuller as a "rare and finished specimen," revealing the greatest "artistic skill." Poe
himself predicted that his poem would "be beheld,
shining above them all as a diamond of purest
water."[32]

"The Raven" presents a poetic mystery in which
suspense, vocalization, and rhythm are operational
at all times. In the essay "The Philosophy of Composition," Poe wrote that he had composed the poem
slowly and arduously, constantly striving for clarity
and logic in the construction of his images and
thoughts. It was not the result of "ecstatic intuition"
or of "fine frenzy" alone.

It is my design to render it manifest that no one point in
its composition is referable either to accident or intuition—
that the work proceeded, step by step, to its completion
with the precision and rigid consequences of a mathematical problem.

Some scholars feel, however, that Poe exaggerated
the point in order to make certain of the rational nature of the work. Certainly intuition was present, as
was "fine frenzy," at least in the initial phase of the
creative endeavor.

"The Raven" is essentially dramatic. A young
scholar is busily occupied over his books, attempting
to learn. He is preoccupied not only with factual information but also with "forgotten lore," indicating
the traditional and historical nature of his interests.

The world of myths and legends, where imagination and the atemporal sphere play such important roles, now takes precedence for the student. He becomes excited at the thought of unknown vistas, and he seemingly dreams as reverie, fancy, unknown and perfumed climes overtake the rational path.

The narrator's study, a circumscribed area, is reminiscent of a prison in the sense that Plato's allegory of the cave was a limiting spatial area representing both the private and the collective spheres. It is within the room, which we may consider symbolically as both the conscious and unconscious realm, that feelings, thoughts, and sensations gestate. The room, a symbolic image of the container, like the brain which is a repository for riches, imposes indwelling; then will the treasures within be subsumed. But there is also something else preoccupying the student: the love he has once known, the beautiful maiden who has died. Will he ever see her again? Will her spirit be accessible to him?

The room, which Poe described as a "close circumscription of space" in "The Philosophy of Composition," is "absolutely necessary" to isolate the incident, to close it off, to contain and frame it. It functions as a *temenos*, a sacred area where "indisputable moral power" exists and forces its attention on the poet, compelling him to concentrate on the inner world where past and present fuse. Confined in the room are, Poe wrote, "Memories of her who had frequented it." These memories are real presences, arousing untold and mysterious psychic patterns, each of which works on the student's soul and body in strange hallucinatory ways. They foster an unquenchable desire to know and thus to be relieved of the great enigma that plagues him: whether in some supernal sphere he will see his beloved again.

Eagerly I wished the morrow;—vainly I had sought to
  borrow
From my books surcease of sorrow—sorrow for the lost
  Lenore—
For the rare and radiant maiden whom the angels name
  Lenore—
  Nameless *here* for evermore.

The objects in the narrator's richly furnished room
exist in our three-dimensional world where time is
instrumental in perpetuating death's jarring feelings.
But the partitions—the curtains, shutters, doors,
windows—attempting to separate the known from
the unknown, consciousness from the irrational
world, will be dealt with as the mystery proceeds.

The time is midnight, as it is in "The Sleeper,"
marking that halfway period between the finite and
the infinite, the inner and outer realm, the median
that cuts through the circle, attempting to sever the
chronological world from the atemporal domain.

The month is December, preceding the new
year that gives the living the illusion of renewal, of
wiping the slate clean and starting anew. For the
ancient Romans, however, December was the tenth
month, since for them the start of the year occurred
in March. It was the month of great coldness and
darkness, as it is for the narrator, who feels warmed
only by the ghostly shadows emanating from the
"dying embers" burning on his hearth. Johannes
Kepler, whom Poe so admired, believed that the
phenomenological sphere could be determined
through the inner world, that within man there
therefore exists the idea of the zodiac and time—of
the cosmos at large—before this emerged into the
conscious sphere and was divided into months,
signs, and symbols, further diversifying what had
once been One and God.

The warmth of the fire, the fatigue from his intellectual pursuits, and the pain of his great loss

cause the narrator to doze. During these moments of slumber, when the world of reality recedes and the invisible takes precedence, dreams and fancies are activated. The scholar-student has withdrawn from the light of consciousness into the darkness of night and the irrational domain, his thoughts reverting to death. He is awakened by a strange noise, "As of some one gently rapping, rapping at my chamber door."

He is startled and looks around at objects in the room that are, psychologically speaking, projections from his unconscious, each evoking specific sensations and thoughts. They are alive and activate something within him, and in this regard they take on the qualities of hierophanies (sacred objects), each endowed with a sacred value since his beloved once touched and moved among them.

As the narrator observes the "dying embers," his mind becomes occupied with mundane questions, partially forgetting "the sorrow for the lost Lenore," that "radiant maiden" who lives on in him as an objective essence or form, an idea to be perpetually recalled in his memory. The fact that he recollects—to use Plato's word for awakening an individual into an existence where past, present, and future coexist—prepares him for the next step in the initiatory process, the "gathering-in" sequence alluded to by Gnostics and Kabbalists.

Lenore went through the depersonalization process when she died as a human being and was reborn as an image; she was divested of her earthly identity forever and remains "Nameless *here* for evermore." But she is a presence, a force, an energetic factor that arouses the narrator's psyche and transforms him in the process from rational scholar delving into his books, firmly entrenched in the temporal world, though dabbling in legend and folklore too, thus conjuring up the imaginative domain. Now, however, he takes a leap into the irrational, the world of poet and mystic, and apocalyptic visions emerge in rapid sequence.

The reader's emotional participation is assured by Poe's use of vocalization, imagery, repetition, internal rhyme, alliteration, onomatopoeia, and color; the visions taking on frightening dimensions as he sees "fantastic terrors" roaming about him. His fierce feelings add to the dread that floods his being. Unknown and fearsome forms seem to advance toward him and then flow about. He hears the "rustling" of the curtains. It must be a visitor, he thinks, returning suddenly to the world of reality, or so he believes. Wondering where the "tapping" came from, he flings open the door. The night is "tempestuous," in sharp contrast "with the [physical] serenity within the chamber." The narrator speaks into the darkness; half humorously, half seriously, he questions the identity of the intruder:

Deep into that darkness peering, long I stood
    there wondering, fearing,
Doubting, dreaming dreams no mortal ever dared
    to dream before;
But the silence was unbroken, and the stillness gave
    no token,
And the only word there spoken was the whispered
    word, "Lenore?"
This I whispered, and an echo murmured back the
    word "Lenore!"

The atmosphere is now charged. The earthbound world seems to have receded into some remote area. The scholar takes a leap into the unknown when he realizes that his books no longer can guide him. His imagination holds full sway; his senses beckon him on to atemporal dimensions, to a void, an abyss, an emptiness. Eternal loss and absence seem to be recapitulated in the soundless utterance of the whispered name "Lenore."

The narrator returns to his room, his mind ablaze, troubled by the noise which gnaws at his inner self imperceptibly, furtively, yet steadily. The reverie at the outset of the poem has incited contents within his subliminal realm, frightening, painful visions as the logical and rational domain recedes.

The door opened by the scholar into the outside world has yielded nothing. Another domain needs to be explored if he is to discover something about his lost love. He then "flung" open the shutter. To his amazement, there stood a raven[33]—an archaic spirit from the past, from the world of folklore and myth.

In there stepped a stately Raven of the saintly days of
    yore.
Not the least obeisance made he; not a minute stopped
    or stayed he;
But, with mien of lord or lady, perched above my
    chamber door—
Perched upon a bust of Pallas just above my chamber
    door—
        Perched, and sat, and nothing more.

As the narrator opens the shutter, so he opens his soul to the outside world. The raven perches on a bust of Pallas's head. The image of Pallas, the goddess of wisdom and the patroness of the arts, titular deity of Athens, was chosen, Poe wrote, because it was "most in keeping with the scholarship of the lover, and, secondly, for the sonorousness of the word, Pallas, itself." The raven then is perched above wisdom; like fate, he dictates all future events. Considered a bird of ill omen because of its black plumage, the raven is also a harbinger of death. Its lugubrious croak echoes sorrowfully throughout the atmosphere and reveals the pain engendered by its solitude, its alienation from the collective, feelings that the student-poet knows well as does many a

creative individual who lives on a plane superior to
that of the crowd. The raven is associated by alchemists with the month of December, which is, as already noted, when the action of the poem takes
place, the most glacial and darkest of months. It is
a time when life draws inward and the outside world
lies barren and destitute. In that the raven flies high
in the sky, it is considered a spiritual force endowed
with divinatory powers and perspicuity as well. It
was a raven that Noah first sent out during the flood
to see if the waters were receding. As such, the raven
is a messenger, a mediator between the known and
the unknown, being and nonbeing, created and uncreated, human and divine. Poe chose the image of
the raven, he wrote, because it was a bird that au-
gured ill and fitted perfectly with "the most poetical
of topics—Death," particularly the death of a beautiful woman.

The narrator is startled by the sight. Frightened
at first by the "ominous reputation of the fowl," he
gathers his courage together and begins to question
it, at first arrogantly and then sardonically.

"Ghastly grim and ancient Raven wandering from the
    Nightly shore—
Tell me what thy lordly name is on the Night's
    Plutonian shore!"
    Quoth the Raven "Nevermore."

Seeking a solution to his despair, the student believes, Poe wrote, "in the prophetic and demoniac
character of the bird." Interestingly, the "Nevermore" which is repeated at the end of each stanza
throughout the rest of the poem becomes very nearly
a comforting sound, as though by the very nature of
its repetition it ushers in a mood of permanence,
"the most delicious because the most intolerable of
sorrow." Despair is exteriorized in the refrain; the

"Nevermore" takes on a cumulative power like a threnody that fleshes out pain and prolongs the ominous mood. The bird is in effect clawing at the student's heart, forcing him by the very nature of his enigmatic replies to face his inner desolation, the negative world in which he is submerged.

The student, dissatisfied with the one-word answer from the raven, confronts the bird, almost jesting this time; "fantastic" and "ludicrous," he describes his quest. Nevertheless, the narrator marvels at the bird, the vision provoked by its presence. Terrifying though it may be, it is still unique. He demands to know more. Will he "meet his mistress in another world?" His whole being is excited at the thought, his mind energized, his pen empowered with creative élan. Again comes the same refrain, the monotonous song that lulls, cajoles, lures the imagination into immeasurable realms. Slowly the world of reality fades, and the raven's "fiery eyes" sear and "burned into my bosom's core." Leaning back on a cushion, the narrator dreams anew:

This and more I sat divining, with my head at ease reclining
On the cushion's velvet lining that the lamp-light gloated o'er,
But whose velvet-violet lining with the lamp-light gloating o'er,
    She shall press, ah, nevermore!

Slowly the shape of the room alters; the atmosphere grows dim and strange, as though the entire vision were hallucinatory: "Then, he thought, the air grew denser, perfumed from an unseen censer," and the raven takes on the dimensions of a seraph, the highest of the nine orders of angels. From his regal height he sits and taunts the student. An evil force now seems to have permeated the atmosphere, whittled it away into the student's inner world, bringing back all the anguish and sorrow of the death of his beloved. "Wretch," he calls the raven, and begs for "respite and nepenthe" (the drug that according to the ancient Greeks caused forgetfulness). The raven has now taken on the dimensions of Satan himself, bearing nothing but hopelessness and doom.

Emotions reach a crescendo as the student's chaotic and tempestuous inner world replaces formerly peaceful cerebral spheres. He needs a balm against his passion, to heal the wound made with the passing of his radiant angelic maiden love. Will he ever see her again? Will love, the root of his inspiration, be his once more? Will it foster the climate necessary to carry him into that purest and rarest of states—from perception to creation—so that he will feel the tingle of the universal flow about him?

The raven only continues to answer, "Nevermore," and in desperation, the narrator shrieking out his rage tries to drive the bird away: "Get thee back into the tempest and the Night's Plutonian shore!" He wants only to wipe out all memory of this apparition and continues: "Leave no black plume as a token of that lie thy soul hath spoken!" But the raven does not leave and "still is sitting, *still* is sitting. / On the pallid bust of Pallas just above my chamber door." Each time the narrator sees it and peers into its lidded eyes—those orbs gazing into a region far beyond that of human understanding—terror floods his entire being. The mystery of life and death and of the creative process as well will never be resolved.

And my soul from out that shadow that lies floating on the floor
Shall be lifted—nevermore!

Poe frequently read "The Raven" when he lec-
tured in public and, because he had such an acute
sense of the dramatic, brought out its very special
melody and mystery. Elmira Royster Shelton, who
listened to him give such a reading in 1849, described it as follows:

When Edgar read "The Raven" he became so wildly excited that he frightened me—when I remonstrated he re-
plied that he could not help it, that it set his brain on
fire.[34]

Another lady present described Poe's recital as for-
midably suspenseful, as if he wanted to stage "The
Raven" as a dramatic ritual.

He would turn down the lamps till the room was almost
dark, then standing in the centre of the apartment he
would recite those wonderful lines in the most melodious
of voices; gradually becoming more and more enthused
. . . he forgot time, spectators, his personal identity. . . . To
the listeners came the sounds of falling rain and waving
branches; the Raven flapped his dusky wings above the
bust of Pallas, and the lovely face of Lenore appeared to
rise before them. So marvelous was his power as a reader
that the auditors would be afraid to draw breath lest the
enchanted spell be broken.[35]

"Ulalume" (1847)

"Ulalume" has been called one of Poe's most lyrical
works. Like a vocal composition it seems actually to
intone feelings of sadness and to take the very character of that emotion itself. It was composed not long
after Virginia's death, when Poe had walked to Ma-
maroneck, New York, about a dozen miles from his
Fordham home, and came to the private cemetery
of the Guion family; the sight of the tombstones and

the pine trees that lined both sides of the drive absorbed his attention fully and completely, and it is there that the poem is set.

Onomastically, the word "ulalume" may be derived from the Latin *ulalure,* meaning "to wail," and the noun *lumen,* signifying light. The very word evokes the wanted mood of mournful sadness and tender understanding.

A mourner is gazing upon what may well be a real landscape as the poem begins, but as is always the case with Poe, it is essentially imaginary. The mourner looks up toward the heavens above, his heart pounding with troubled pain. The trees on both sides of the path insulate and isolate him, protecting him from intruding glances, but try also to keep him from looking outward. Rapturously he seems to behold the cosmos above, taking it in in an exalted embrace.

> The skies they were ashen and sober;
>   The leaves they were crispéd and sere—
>   The leaves they were withering and sere;

The month is October, the beginning of harvest and the end of any hope of further warm summer months. The atmosphere is melancholy as nature lies dying all about. The trees, once green and full of leaves, are bare, standing like skeletal forces silhouetted against a pale and endless sky. The earth, covered with dead leaves, lies dormant, in keeping with the narrator's entire outlook, as if it were mourning with him for his beloved.

The mourner walks about distressed. We realize, however, that he is not wholly alone and abandoned when he begins conversing with Psyche, the soul or anima figure who is the personification of womankind for him, the friend and adviser who

warms his cold spirit and has helped him to accept
his solitude.

Mist veils the atmosphere, reminiscent, Poe
suggests, of the canvases of Robert Walter Weir of
the Hudson River school of painters, known for his
vague misty landscapes, in which the eye can barely
make out anything but sequences of shadows and
suggestive sensations. The poem is flooded with
subdued emotions. A "ghoul-haunted woodland"
with its tortuous shapes now takes over, rising
seemingly above the narrator from all sides. Accompanied with these pictorial visions are aural litanies,
reminiscent of the operas of Esprit Auber, the
nineteenth-century writer of witty, tuneful, and sophisticated operas, a precursor of impressionistic
music who broke down tonality, paving the way for
mood music.

The lake is dim, the woodlands dank and dreary.
The narrator thinks back to his youth, when passion
surged and his heart pounded, restless and tumul-
tuous. He compares his feelings to a volcano: "the
lavas that restlessly roll," ejecting their "sulphurous
currents down Yaanek," which has been identified
with Mount Erebus, a volcanic mountain in Antarc-
tica.

Psyche leads him on, preventing him from becoming suffocated by his searing feelings. She is
"serious and sober" and forbids him to sentimen-
talize his past, advising him not to squander such
depth of feeling on fleeting facile emotions; to do
so is sinful and is certain to render superficial all
his poetical flights.

The mourner recalls his lost love. When she was
alive, he did not realize that death was so near, that
night with its blackness would call her days to a halt.
A chill permeated the air, he recalls, as he pursues

his walk along the dimly lit pathway. It created havoc with his love who was so frail and beauteous.
Soon he sees "star-dials pointed to morn," and unfamiliar sensations encroach.

> And nebulous lustre was born,
> Out of which a miraculous crescent
> Arose with a duplicate horn—
> Astarte's bediamonded crescent
> Distinct with its duplicate horn.

He looks at Astarte's light, and its beauty en-
trances him and benumbs his senses. The Phoeni-
cian goddess Astarte corresponds to the Babylonian
Ishtar and to the Roman Venus, all considered the
most beautiful of celestial bodies and referred to as
the Queen of Heaven. The goddess of love and war,
the mother of mankind, each attained primacy as the
feminine source of sexual life and the personification
of that creative force in nature. Astarte, however, was
condemned by the biblical Hebrews, who were for-
bidden even to pronounce her name; the world she
evoked was sensual, unpredictable, and ungodly.

The narrator is captivated by the sight of Astarte;
as she blazes in the heavens, she symbolizes another,
different sort of love. She evokes sensuality, passion,
and warmth, far more enticing to him physically than
his first love, Diana.

But Psyche raises her finger. "Sadly this star I
mistrust," she tells him. Its "pallor" is inexplicable,
and she hastens to leave and encourages him to follow her. The narrator wants, however, to pursue his
course, excited at the thought of "this tremulous
light" offering him its "Sibyllic splendor," a new
world of fantasy and illusion, "with Hope and in
beauty to-night." Psyche hesitates, convinced that
Astarte is an intruder, a destructive force, hiding and
veiling truth and fidelity of feeling.

> Thus I pacified Psyche and kissed her,
>   And tempted her out of her gloom—

Guilt obtrudes, however. The mourner has ne-
glected his first love, has even forgotten that it was
on this very night just a year before that he buried
what he most cherished. In agony now, he stops at
the "door of the tomb" and questions Psyche:

> "What is written, sweet sister,
> On the door of this legended tomb?"
> She replied—"Ulalume—Ulalume—
> 'T is the vault of thy lost Ulalume!"

Memories flow forth; human shapes burden the
atmosphere and infiltrate the landscape, deadening
feeling; the atmosphere grows progressively more
remote and unreal. Any further identification with
nature ceases: "Then my heart it grew ashen and
sober," as the mourner cries out his grief, recalling
the date of his great loss and facing his feelings and
acts.

Her name is Ulalume, he wails and bewails. A
presence is felt, an essence, emerging into the chill
night air; a sacred force seems to take over the proceedings. The tomb and the vault, containing devices that provoke thoughts of death and frozenness
of being, evoke an entire spectral realm. The dim-
ness of the light underscores the macabre and phan-
tasmal mood: "From the limbo of lunary souls."
Tears flow as the narrator confesses his inability to
live unless he acknowledges the grave-sepulcher,
his need to recollect those beautiful moments he
once knew, always to have them and relive them, if
only in his mind.

> That I journeyed—I journeyed down here—
> That I brought a dread burden down here—
> On this night of all nights in the year,
> Ah, what demon has tempted me here?

The narrator is simultaneously lover and mourner, accuser and victim; his feelings that have been imprisoned now flow forth in the misty grave-yard region, this "ghoul-haunted woodland." In ter-ror he has roamed about attempting to exteriorize his fears and torments in lyrical lamentations, earn-ing release from the burdens of "this sinfully scin-tillant planet," this second love that has so caught his fancy and subjugated his senses. Yet the mourner knows that his first great love—the one who lies in the grave, whom Psyche has tried to protect by speaking to the mourner, thereby recalling the image of his beloved to his conscious mind—must always remain his beloved. Ulalume—that poetic force—sings forth her lament through him; she keeps alive his sorrow, but she also is what inspires, as in the past, and will continue to inspire his poetical pow-ers.

"Such was the poet's lonely midnight walk," wrote Mrs. Sarah Helen Whitman, the widow to whom Poe was engaged for a brief period in 1848. As the narrator continues on the path, "Amid the desolate memories and sceneries of the hour," a "newborn hope enkindled within his heart at the sight of the morning star—" And when he saw "As-tarte's bediamond crescent" coming up as the beau-tiful harbinger of love and happiness, his feelings of rapture suddenly turned to "dread," for in that moment he discovered what had gone unnoticed at first—that Astarte shone "as if in mockery or in warning, directly over the sepulcher of the lost 'Ulalume' "[36] Poe too realized in the empirical do-main that whoever his new love might be, his single great passion, Virginia, would always be there wait-ing, watching, observing, preventing him from sin-gling out anyone else during the years to come.

"The Bells" (1849)

Of all Poe's poems, "The Bells" is particularly marked by its unusual tonal and rhythmic effects. The theme was suggested to Poe by Marie Louise Shew, who had helped to care for Virginia during her last illness, as she was later to do for Poe himself. Both Mrs. Shew and Poe had listened to the chimes of Grace Church in New York City as well as the bells of many other churches and places about the city.

Poe had always been fascinated by bells and chimes, by their metallic sonorities, their heighth and depth, and their historicity. Bells appear in some of his stories, including "The Masque of the Red Death." In "The Bells," there is a similar feeling of dread interspersed with excitement as the world at large is evoked and the sound of the bells fills the air.

In addition to the onomatopoeia that Poe so effectively uses to evoke harsh, mellifluous, jarring, loving, and cajoling sounds, the repetition of the word "bells" prolongs its sonorities and rhythms. Bells underscore a time factor in Poe's verses; they toll out the hours of the day, of life. More specifically, they mark the four ages of man: the silver bells pealing out youth and merriment; the golden bells, happiness and harmony in love and marriage; and the brazen bells, maturity and the realization of the polarities and dichotomies in life and the struggle between good and evil. The iron bells ring out for old age—death and the next step onward.

> Keeping time, time, time,
> In a sort of Runic rhyme,
>   To the throbbing of the bells—

Of the bells, bells, bells—
   To the sobbing of the bells:—
Keeping time, time, time
   As he knells, knells, knells,
In a happy Runic rhyme,
   To the rolling of the bells—
   Of the bells, bells, bells:—
   To the tolling of the bells—
Of the bells, bells, bells, bells,
   Bells, bells, bells—
To the moaning and the groaning of the bells.

The technical and mechanical devices used by Poe, the prolongation and shortening of such vowel sounds as *i, o, u,* the use of consonants, nasals, and liquids, underscoring as they do certain tonalities and rhythmic effects, engage the reader in an emotional interchange. The ideas in "The Bells" are of secondary importance. What is significant is the stressed, catching, pounding rhythm and the shifting melodious sonorities that give the poem its remarkably dramatic auditory effect.

"Annabel Lee" (1849)

"Annabel Lee," perhaps more than any other of Poe's poems, should be read aloud to be fully appreciated, for its tones and timbres, meter and metrics, for the flow of the feelings involved. The six stanzas of "Annabel Lee," a tale of loss and of pain which lives on eternally beyond death, lull the reader into a bygone period, into a "kingdom by the sea," there to be absorbed into a sequence of hypnotic rhythms. Although reminiscent of "Lenore," the auditive effects are simpler here, mounting in depth and poignancy to the final crescendo.

The narrator recollects his beloved whose life was centered on him.

> It was many and many a year ago,
>   In a kingdom by the sea
> That a maiden there lived whom you may know
>   By the name of ANNABEL LEE:
> And this maiden she lived with no other thought
>   Than to love and be loved by me.

The poet recounts their joys when they were children and re-creates a world of rapture and fantasy in which they dwelled. Nature in all her guises is evoked, sensualized, and concretized. That Poe should have chosen the seashore as the setting for the poem, dealing with what he most cherished, indicates the depth of his projection on to this life-giving element without which nothing else would exist. Limitless and immortal, water is the beginning and end of all things; it represents the container and the contained, that is, love. Although formless, like love it is always shifting and changing, infiltrating into every natural force, coloring vision and feeling. Water, as earlier discussed, existing as it does in the physical world and contained in vapor, mist, cloud formations, also represents a potential world, dynamic yet unformed. It is the element that fosters and protects the fetus and from which new life emerges. In the same way that water purifies and intensifies the numinosity of love, so it clarifies, reflects, and refracts emotion.

Water can mean the end of human life, as when Charon rows his boat across the River Styx, taking the dead to the other side, or when Ophelia drowns herself in her watery grave. But for the narrator, the "kingdom by the sea" was joy, that time when he and the beloved were children together. And then came that wintry squall, which chilled and clouded the atmosphere, leading to the death of his love, shutting her up in "a sepulchre" far and yet close to him, in that spaceless and timeless region of the soul, his home now, where he recollects the past and integrates it into his present.

The endless rhythm of the waves of the sea summons memories of a pure joy so intense that perhaps even angels were jealous of feelings that no earthly or unearthly force could dispel. Nothing could deaden the feelings the two felt for one another or "dissever my soul from the soul" of the beautiful Annabel Lee.

> And so, all the night-tide, I lie down by the side
> Of my darling—my darling—my life and my bride,
>   In the sepulchre there by the sea—
>   In her tomb by the sounding sea.

Unrivaled in beauty and feeling, even by Novalis's *Hymns to the Night*, Poe's marriage—no matter what its physical earthly facts—was consummated in subliminal spheres in "Annabel Lee," the watery depths of his unconscious activating his visions and visitations.

Poe's prerequisite for art was purity, truth, the contemplation of beauty in the ascension of the soul to supernal spheres. In such poems as "Al Aaraaf," "To Helen," "The Sleeper," "The Raven," "Ulalume," "Lenore," and "Annabel Lee," he reached out to those heights attainable only in "brief and indeterminate glimpses,"[37] and there he created his works of art. Simple and direct, his diction lulls as it personifies; its rhythmic melodious repetitions of protracted vowel sounds and consonants lodge deep within the reader's mind and spirit. It is perhaps in Poe's lamentations for lost love that he is at his best, drawing on his technical resources and emotional depth to create the lyrical equivalent of the mood he seeks to convey. As the word is unleashed in the verse, washed of earthly dross, divested of mundane chatter and clatter, cut free from the volatile world of contingencies, it ascends to collective spheres, endowing the subject, be it beauty or the mourning lover, with archetypal force.

Poe the mystic was able to give his songs and dirges eternality, for they are concerned with the most timeless area of all, that of the human heart.

4

The Tales

It is this admirable and immortal instinct for the beautiful which causes us to consider the earth and its wonders as a revelation, as a correspondence with Heaven. The insatiable thirst for all that lies beyond, and what life reveals, is the most vital proof of our immortality. It is at once by poetry and *through* poetry, by and *through* music, that the soul glimpses the splendors beyond the tomb; and, when we are moved to tears by an exquisite poem, those tears are not the result of excessive joy, they are instead testimony to an inflamed melancholy, demanding nerves, a nature exiled in imperfection, and which seeks to possess, at once, on this very earth, a paradise revealed.

Charles Baudelaire, *New Notes on Edgar Poe.*

Poe's tales of horror, terror, and the supernatural may be regarded as descents into an interior inferno, a bleak, dank, fungal realm often replete with dungeon cells and torture chambers. Psychologically, they are probings into the unsounded depths of the collective unconscious, the very heart of mystery and of being. For the creative writer, the blackness experienced in those depths may be likened to that of primal void, that period described in Genesis as existing prior to the Creation: "And the earth was without form and void; and darkness was on the face of the deep." It is from this primal source that the new, the untried, the unknown is brought forth. The seed of the yet to be created form gestates and develops within these depths in the same way that the fetus does within the uterus, growing and finally emerging into the clarity of consciousness in the written word or work of art, from darkness into light.

Historically, the short story as a form dates back at least to the Bible, to the Book of Ruth, the Book of Daniel, and many more. In medieval times Chaucer's *The Canterbury Tales* and Boccaccio's *Decameron* used this genre. During the Renaissance, Marguerite de Navarre's *Heptameron* regaled countless readers, and so, during the seventeenth, eighteenth, and nineteenth centuries, did the works of Swift, Defoe—who was the creator of the first modern ghost stories—Sade, Diderot, Dickens, Balzac, E. T. A. Hoffmann, Brentano, Arnim, Flaubert, Nerval, and Maupassant.

Poe, however, was an innovator. The inventor of those modern brands of short stories that include science fiction and the detective story, he also explored the world of nightmare and delved, as Charles Baudelaire noted, into the "secret chambers of the mind." Unlike his poetry, which deals with supernal spheres, many of Poe's fictional works focus on grotesque and fantastic events, emotionally deformed and eccentric beings. Some of Poe's protagonists suffer from psychological disorders; many of his feminine characters are possessed of a "monstrous will and intellect" and dominate their male counterparts before all are reduced to ashes. J. K. Huysmans wrote that no one was better versed than Poe in the "realm of morbid psychology" or more fascinated by that complex "region of the will."[1] Poe's protagonists are obsessed with death, by the fear of being buried alive; others waste away for no apparent reason, the body victimized by a pathological condition.

The scenes and settings that Poe devises for these tales are fitting backdrops for his ghouls and ghostly emanations and augment the sense of mystery and suspense. In "Ligeia," for example, he describes the bridal chamber with such vivid attention to material detail that the closed curtains of crimson silk, the folds of the fabric, and the forms and circular shadows that they cast become in themselves reflections of the emotional state of the characters. In "The Masque of the Red Death," seven different colors are used to relate the slow encroachment and inexorable advance of death. Poe's fascination with physical setting, including eerie lighting effects, prepares the reader for the harrowing events to come. It is interesting to recollect that Poe was the son of actors and that he himself had completed three "dialogues" of a play, *Politan*, and was the drama critic of the *Broadway Journal*.

Poe's *Tales of the Grotesque and Arabesque* (1840) conjure forth a strange and chilling world filled with blendings of human and nonhuman beings, highly imaginative and often bizarre and incongruous. Poe chose the title for this collection from two styles of decorative ornamentation. The word "grotesque" is derived from the Italian *grottesca*, identified with those unrepresentational Italian "grotto paintings" that blended persons and animals with foliage, flowers, and fruits in fantastic designs, thereby creating overfanciful and overelaborate settings antithetical to the well-ordered and rational sphere. A weird, distorted, tormented Gothic quality was soon grafted onto the style, as can be seen, for example, in Breughel and Bosch's frightening eidetic images—early examples of what has come to be known as black humor. The word "arabesque," on the other hand, stems from Arabic designs, from those highly ornamental, intertwining geometrically

abstract patterns used in connection with ribbed
vaulting, pointed arches, and soaring turrets and
minarets.[2] Imaginative profusion and complexity are
evident here in both styles as opposed to the rule
and order found in the classical Western outlook.
For Poe, then, the title represented in part the rest-
lessness and extreme mental agitation of his intense,
overwrought characters; but the tales include also
much dazzling visual beauty of an edenlike nature
and nearly Utopian quality as in "The Domain of
Arnheim" and "The Island of the Fay." Yet there is
also an almost oppressive as well as delicate feeling
of bewilderment, of strangeness and puzzlement.
Although Poe's characters are varied, they all live
inwardly and rarely look outward; it is the interior
mystery of the mind that he probes and dramatizes.

Poe was influenced by both the Gothic novel
and by the romantic movement that swept over
England and Europe in his day. He was also very
much of an eighteenth-century man, as previously
mentioned, emphasizing logic and reason even
when probing the supernatural world. It is this ability to present an objective assessment of the external
situation in combination with the inner world of his
characters that makes Poe's tales so fascinating. The
objective detailed description of the outside world
gives increased credence to the disintegrating mephitic inner realm, augmenting a hundredfold the
verisimilitude and therefore the horror of the situations disclosed.

Gothic novels in the later eighteenth and early
nineteenth centuries in both Europe and America
were characterized by terror, violence, supernatural
effects, and a taste for medieval architecture, replete
with gloomy castles, trap doors, dungeons, and secret
hiding places. Horace Walpole was the initiator of
the genre. His *Castle of Otranto*, a work replete with

poisonings, prophecies, ghosts, and supernatural
events, took readers by storm. Mistress Ann Radcliffe
then added her adventuresome and melancholy sequences to this new kind of entertainment in *The
Mysteries of Udolpho*, a work abounding in perse-
cutions, romantic escapes, marriages, and mysterious
births, always realistically described. William
Beckford's *Vathek* included sorceresses, pacts with
the devil, torture chambers, infernal fires, and a pre-
Adamite sultan. Matthew Gregory Lewis's *The Monk*
introduced readers to even more mental frissons,
with crime after crime taking place in remote underground regions.

The British Gothic novel had its American
counterparts. Charles Brockden Brown created
deeply psychotic and cruelly vicious characters in
Wieland, or The Transformation, dealing with a
sinister ventriloquist and his nefarious influence on
a Pennsylvania family of German mystics. William
Gilmore Simms, although more generally identified
as the author of southern plantation novels, also
wrote ghost stories. His *Castle Dismal* was characterized by Poe "as one of the most original fictions
ever penned and deserves all the order of com-
mendation which the critics lavished upon Walpole's
Castle of Otranto."[3] Hawthorne, whose ancestors
had played a part in the Salem witch trials, explored
the notion of sin in a fanatic Puritan society. Hawthorne's *Twice-Told-Tales*, Poe noted, "belong to the
highest region of Art—an Art subservient to genius
of a very lofty order."[4] *The Tales of a Traveller* by
Washington Irving were also praised by Poe because
they combined satire and whimsy; they were
"graceful and impressive narratives."[5]

The novelists and poets affected Poe's tale-tell-
ing technique. Sir Walter Scott, for example, known
for his *Waverley* novels, created atmosphere and por-

trayed characters in a world filled with marvelously thrilling incidents set against an authentic historical background. Poe must have had these works in mind when composing his "Von Kempelen and His Discoveries" and "Ligeia." Thomas Moore, the Irish poet known for his graceful lyrics and folk songs, may have inspired Poe to introduce certain lyrical sequences of enchanting quality into "The Colloquy of Monos and Una" and "The Island of the Fay." So did the works of the other writers—Coleridge, Byron, Shelley, and Keats—make their impress on him.

German mysticism and philosophy also interested Poe intensely. Schlegel, Fichte, Hegel, Schelling, and Kant made inroads onto Poe's works, as will be discussed in the last chapter. Interesting to Poe as well were the writings of the *Sturm und Drang*, with their storm and stress, their intensity of feeling, and alienation from society: Friedrich Schiller's tragedy *Love and Intrigue* (1784) with its jealousies and schemings; Goethe's *The Sorrows of Young Werther* (1774) and the theme of unrequited love and suicide; Heinrich von Kleist's *Penthesilea* (1808), with its exhilarations and plunges of feelings and their pernicious power; Novalis's *Hymns to the Night* (1800), expressing his yearnings for death and burial in mystical modes.

Tales dealing with the supernatural sphere, with nightmares, sleepwalking, clairvoyance, telepathic communication, perception, pacts with the devil, and dabblings in witchcraft flooded the continent and were instrumental in helping Poe to burnish his initial conceptions. *Siebenkäs* (1796–97) by Jean-Friedrich Richter dealt with a sensitive husband who ends his unhappy marriage by feigning death and burial. Coleridge, who took drugs, claimed that the dream was at the origin of his "Kubla Khan"

(1797); De Quincey's *Confessions of an English Opium-Eater*; Blake's *The Marriage of Heaven and Hell* (1790) and his visionary material with its doctrine of opposites all stimulated Poe's imagination. Nor may we omit the French writers of this period: Charles Nodier's *Smarrah* (1822), which introduced readers to a world of dreams and sorceresses; Victor Hugo's *Notre Dame de Paris* (1831) and its alchemists and gypsies; Gérard de Nerval's *The Enchanted Hand*, with its dual personality; Balzac's forays into madness in *Louis Lambert* (1832), and many more contributions in the domain of the irrational.

But although Poe was conversant with the daemons of other writers, he was clearly very much an artist in his own right, eager and ready to confront the topography of his own subjective personality in all its emotional chaos as well as its artful and faultless logic. "Originality," he wrote in "The Philosophy of Composition," "is by no means a matter, as some suppose of impulse or intuition. In general, to be found, it must be elaborately sought, and although a positive merit of the highest class demands in its attainment less of invention than negation."

Poe was a stylist who worked for unity of effect, slowly, painstakingly, methodically dissecting his characters' needs and conditions with the objectivity of a scientist. The minute, pictorially true details he includes in his works seem at times comparable to the conspicuous realism of such painters as Dürer, Bosch, and Breughel.

Whatever the theme that Poe chose to explore, whether in the tales of infernal or paradisiacal realms; the detective stories with their clear-cut directness, their deductive reasoning power, their "ratiocinations"; or in those science fiction tales with their insights into unknown worlds and premonitory

nings, there is always a remarkable unity of
.t, an intensity that ignites and grows, as though
entire scheme of things had been structured in
oₙₑ swift yet solid movement. In "Tale Writing"
(1842), Poe described his method:

A skilful artist has constructed a tale. He has not fashioned his thoughts to accommodate his incidents, but
having deliberately conceived a certain *single effect* to be
wrought, he then invents such incidents, he then combines
such events, and discusses them in such tone as may best
serve him in establishing this preconceived effect. If his
very first sentence tends not to the out-bringing of this
effect, then in his very first step he has committed a blun-
der. In the whole composition there should be no word
written of which the tendency, direct or indirect, is not
the one pre-established design. And by such means, with
such care and skill, a picture is at length painted which
leaves in the mind of him who contemplates it with a
kindred art, a sense of the fullest satisfaction.

The Descent

Poe's tales of the sea, "MS. Found in a Bottle"
(1833), *The Narrative of Arthur Gordon Pym of
Nantucket* (1838), and "A Descent into the Maelstrom" (1841), are so powerful that they seem to take
on a mythical dimension. The myth, of course, is a
means of coveying a cosmic thought or belief. It
narrates a primordial experience, not necessarily a
personal one but always one that is transpersonal;
not something invented to express an old belief but
rather a living, true, and burning reality existent in
a people's psyche and culture. It is therefore both
ectypal (dealing with the existential world and
chronological or historic time) and archetypal (eternal and timeless, containing past, present, and future
within its scope).

These stories of Poe's take us into a dual realm: the temporal frame of reference in which the narrators live in an ego-conscious world, preoccupied with mundane and personal needs; and the atemporal, concerned with archaic and perhaps outworn forces prevailing within the individual and the society of which he is a part. Transpersonal creatures are featured in Poe's tales; they struggle to bring about a collective view and to tap universal and eternal forces, and in so doing, they attain expanded consciousness. Poe's frames of reference are thereby enriched by dual values and dual sets of priorities and insights. But these are not necessarily integrated into the personality of his protagonists. More frequently than not, his narrators are passive, one-sided, and ailing, necessitating a return to the primal state, to death for renewal. A dissolution of the ego rather than a strengthening of this center of consciousness occurs, a physical and spiritual loss of identity. Poe's tales of the sea take his reader into an uncharted land where vast physical forces wait for their victim, ready to encircle, entrap, and annihilate him.

Most of the characters in these tales either perish early in life or vanish when they are very old men. Such a fate, however horrifying and unwarranted it seems, may be viewed symbolically as a rite of passage, a means of attaining a needed rebirth. "To die," Plato wrote, "is to be initiated."[6] For Poe such an experience necessitated a plunge into the vortex of nothingness, into that unlimited realm which C. G. Jung refers to as the collective unconscious. Unlike the personal unconscious "which embraces all the acquisitions of the personal existence—hence, the forgotten, the repressed, the subliminally perceived, thought and felt," the collective unconscious refers to the "deepest layer of the un-

conscious which is ordinarily inaccessible to conscious awareness." It is a universal, suprapersonal,
and nonindividual sphere. When, for example, it is
experienced by a person in a dream, the ego—the
center of consciousness—frequently considers it as
something foreign and alien and also as something
numinous or divine.[7]

Poe explores both the personal and the collective unconscious in these tales, marked by horrifying
drowning descents into oceans and seas, shadowy
realms, dark abysses, chambers of his own mind. In
this primal substrata, the reader is exposed to the
dread shudderings of a soul peering into a world
beyond the grave, outside the world of contingencies
yet within it as well, a thinking intellect endowed
with what Poe considered a superior capacity—intuition. This cerebral force makes its way grudgingly
into the lower depths of the very universe itself, the
heaving tidal waters with their immeasurable and
incommensurate whirling eddies and velocities, the
womb, the mother. For the mystic, this is the sole
way of experiencing the One or God.

In these tales, Poe's protagonists gasp for air and
are sucked down by gigantic whirling maelstroms,
searching frantically for something to grab on to, a
force or object that will buoy them up and carry them
to safety. Archetypal images—those "unknown motivating dynamisms of the psyche"—abound as Poe
seeks to re-create the havoc he himself has known,
in the hearts and minds of his readers.[8] The imagery
grows persistently more terrifying as the protagonists
are drawn ever more deeply into unearthly realms.
Nocturnal shadows, night terrors, revenants, spirits
of the dead, prisons, tombs, dismembered beings,
storms, shipwrecks abound, mnemonic images rising
from the prison of Poe's past and his own collective
unconscious.

The immediate source of these tales was often culled from a current newspaper, a magazine article, a story Poe had learned through word of mouth, or a book he had read. The initial anecdote, however, merely provided the underpinning of the work. The cumulative, spectral narrative and the archetypal images generated emanated from his own inner sphere and thus acquired a magnetic and sometimes luminous power. Poe's extreme control over his medium and his objectivity in relating macabre, horrific events underscore the truth and actuality of what seem at the outset impossible situations but which become in the course of the telling not only possible but real.

Water is a dissolving agent; it decomposes and disperses fixed and concrete entities. Therefore, in the psychological realm it separates seemingly sure and secure fixed attitudes, those stumbling blocks that prevent needed interchange between the conscious and the unconscious. One of the four ancient elements, water has always stood for flux and change. Like fire, it is a transitional force, a mediator between life and death.

Water also is associated with the collective unconscious because both are unfathomably deep and unplumbed realms; innumerable riches exist inchoate within their depths. At night, when it is calm, the surface of the water can take on a smooth and glassy sheen, reflecting the stars and planets on its surface, seemingly unifying heaven and earth, the height merged into the depth. Large expanses of the ocean have a hypnotic quality about them, their perpetual movement mesmerizing the beholder; so too archetypal images thrust up from the collective unconscious may haunt and dominate consciousness if concentrated upon for a long period. When the sea is storm-tossed and turbulent, it pounds with

unrelenting, cataclysmic force, often causing destruction and death. Smothered and drowned is the
person who sinks beneath its depths. In the same
way the ego, when overwhelmed by the power and
energy of repressed archetypal images, sometimes
disintegrates into nothingness, swallowed up by the
watery ground bed.

"MS. Found in a Bottle" (1833)

When "MS. Found in a Bottle" was published, Poe
was in desperate straits, living in Baltimore with the
Clemms and having no assurance that he could succeed in his chosen field of literary work. He had
been expelled from West Point in 1830 and greatly
feared that he would be disinherited by his foster
father, John Allan. This was an entirely justifiable
fear, as subsequent events would prove. On April
12, 1833, he wrote John Allan yet another of his
many desperate letters: "It has been more than two
years since you have assisted me, and more than
three since you have spoken to me. I feel little hope
that you will pay any regard to this letter, but still
I cannot refrain from making one more attempt to
interest you in my behalf."[9]
    The story line of "MS. Found in a Bottle" cen-
ters on a young man who comes from a well-to-do
family; he has traveled the world over but has found
no real reason for existence. Deciding to sail the
South Seas, he embarks from Java on a well-fitted
ship. All goes well until one evening an incredible
calm settles down, followed by a terrifying storm.
Everyone on board is swept into the sea except for
an old Swedish sailor and the narrator. Strong winds
blow fearsomely for the next five days as the ship
nears the coast of Australia. "A new sense, a new

identity is added to my soul," the narrator states. The old Swede, a superstitious man, is, however, terrified by the overpowering blackness that isolates the two men in what seems to be a limitless expanse of ocean. Suddenly and without warning, the shadow of a huge ship looms over them, and then the vessel itself bears rapidly down, crashing into them, the shock from the collision catapulting the narrator onto the deck of an alien vessel. The only survivor of the original voyage, he hides in a hatchway to ascertain what the situation is; from there, he observes the crew, all of whom are old, infirm men. When he leaves his hiding place and walks about on deck, no one seems to see him; the members of the crew pass him by without any sign of recognition. He feels as if he were walking among the dead. He makes his way to the captain's private quarters and there starts to write down his thoughts. Everything about the ship, he now realizes, is in a state of decay; even the wood is rotten. The objects in the captain's quarters—the charts and ancient measuring instruments—belong to the days of the Spanish galleons; the captain himself, though steady on his feet, has a "sybil-old" face. As the ship moves on through what appears to be unlimited icy dark, the narrator's thoughts grow increasingly apocalyptic:

We are surely doomed to hover continually upon the brink of Eternity, without taking a final plunge into the abyss. Foam billows a thousand times more stupendous from any I have ever seen, we glide away with the facility of the arrow seagull; and the colossal waters rear their heads above us like demons of the deep . . . (p. 6).

The narrator feels impelled to investigate, "to penetrate the mystery of these awful regions." Despair soon encroaches—that feeling which comes

upon one when one has lost one's bearings, when
unsteadiness of footing takes over. The imagery
grows increasingly terrifying: "The ice opens suddenly to the right, and to the left" of the ship. "We
are whirling, dizzily, in immense concentric circles,
round and round the borders of a gigantic amphi-
theatre, the summit of those walls is lost in the darkness of the distance." Overwhelmed, the narrator
seems to lose all power of expression as the phantom
ship wildly rotates. "We are plunging madly with
the grasp of the whirlpool—and amid a roaring, bel-
lowing, and thundering of ocean and of tempest, the
ship is quivering, oh God! and—going down" are
the last words in Poe's story.

To experience such alienation and horror as
Poe's narrator undergoes in "MS. Found in a Bottle"
represents a deeply felt need for psychological
death, for an eclipse of the ego and a schizophrenic
disintegration of consciousness. Step by step Poe
takes the reader from the realm of the living into a
spectral world of shadows, from the existential
sphere to that of the subliminal universe whose primal waters dissolve and absolve. The constant motion and the explosiveness of energy expressed in
the archetypal imagery finally force matter itself to
disappear, Poe suggested years later in his prose
poem *Eureka*, intuiting in so doing the very notion
of the black hole propounded by today's physicists.
For Poe, the black nothingness that invaded his narrator's mind's eye was an example of "the plainly
inevitable annihilation of at least the material universe" (*Eureka*, p. 227).

The ship, as in so many accounts of voyages from
Homer's *Odyssey* to Katherine Ann Porter's *Ship of
Fools*, may metaphorically represent a human body
or a concrete point of view, an attitude, a way of life.
Poe describes the first ship as being sturdy and well

fitted, worthy of sailing the seven seas. But is it? What is considered structurally solid may be destroyed easily by a powerful encounter, and after the first storm, the ship and all but one of the crew perish. Only the narrator and the superstitious old man remain, who represents those narrow-minded attitudes which the narrator considers inconsistent with the laws of science; he refers to the fact that the Swede is superstitious. With the advent of the second ship, the ship of death, he too will be swept under.

The narrator does his best to make himself at home on what proves to be the ship of death, but he is unable to do so. He cannot communicate with anyone; he simply notes what he sees in the world of the dead and dying. Every person aboard is old, and worn out, like so many spirits that hover about. For the narrator, they represent dead and decayed traditions, outworn values, and presences that soon will be destroyed as they should be in accordance with the death of the old king in ancient primitive societies who must die in order for the kingdom to be restored and revitalized. This second ship, the ship of death, is not described as sturdy, like the first vessel, but as "porous" and waterlogged. The ancestral paternal values that it carries, instead of protecting and guiding the narrator through life's course and helping him acquire some semblance of independence, some consciousness over his own destiny, are "worm-eaten." Its wooden frame is worthless, rotted, and decayed. In this outworn decrepit structure, the narrator feels cut off from life and from consciousness. No relationship can possibly come into being between the narrator and the "gray-haired" captain, who is depicted as sitting amid his charts, reading his instruments. These devices used to chart the ship's direction, are antiquated, no longer in working condition and therefore worthless to the narrator. The captain and the crew are described as "ghosts of buried centuries." Everything about them is strange and wild-eyed, alienating the narrator still further and encouraging him to delve more deeply into his own inner domain.

The written word alone gives the narrator direction; it alone affords him some semblance of the security he so desperately craves, allowing him to clarify his thoughts and bear witness to the creative human spirit. His words alone will survive the watery depths, for they alone give his lost and alienated spirit strength, purpose, and direction. It is not the physical body but the word, the logos, that will outlive the whirlpool.

Whirlpools or whirlwinds frequently occur in creation myths. They are harbingers of the new, of the archetypal image, the fresh vision that presently will emerge from the collective unconscious. Although an uncontrollable cosmic force drags down the narrator to his death, causing the annihilation of his physical being, it does not succeed in destroying the fruit of his conscious volition, his written manuscript. The maelstrom, characterized by its spiral or helical motion, negates physical temporal life but paves the way for entry into timeless spheres. The Hebrew *vav* or the Egyptian hieroglyphic of the spiral represents galactic form in motion, or connotes an identification of unity with multiplicity: consciousness and the unconscious, the created and the uncreated, the known and the unknown. That the manuscript survived, that it was saved, indicates the power and eternality of that creative force within the human being, which includes both temporal and atemporal spheres.

"A Descent into the Maelstrom" (1841)

When "A Descent into the Maelstrom" was published, Poe had assumed the editorship of *Graham's Magazine* in Philadelphia. Although the work was demanding, he was experiencing a highly creative period. The previous year had seen the publication of *Tales of the Grotesque and Arabesque* and "The Murders in the Rue Morgue," and he was developing further a relatively new interest, the solving of ciphers and the exploration of the world of cryptography.

The basis for "A Descent into the Maelstrom" may have come from an article Poe read in *Alexander's Weekly Messenger* in 1838, which described the vast Drontheim whirlpool; supplemental readings in the *Encyclopaedia Britannica* may have filled in what Poe himself did not know about such a force from a technical point of view. The tale itself, which is recounted by the sole survivor of the ghastly incident, is harrowing. The narrator, a Norwegian fisherman, has often sailed out to sea successfully with his two brothers. On this occasion, however, a whirlpool or maelstrom (known as "the Moskoeström") strikes. Its terrifying wind of "monstrous velocity" rocks the ship. Although the three young men do their best to steer the vessel clear of the whirlpool's apocalyptic force, they are unable to do so.

Here the vast bed of the waters, seamed and scarred into a thousand conflicting channels, burst suddenly into phrensied convulsions—heaving, boiling, hissing—gyrating in gigantic and innumerable vortices, and all whirling and plunging into the eastward with a rapidity which water never elsewhere assumes except in precipitous descents (p. 270).

There is something sacred and numinous in Poe's description of the wind and the sea, as if the turbulent vortex of water and the cyclonic wind had been conjured up by the very elements themselves, water and air contending. In the Bible, rushing wind represents the supernal spirit, the same spirit that God breathed into Adam's nostrils. It is the cosmic spirit in "A Descent into the Maelstrom" which blows and engulfs all living things, eradicating the orientation of the fishermen and later destroying their lives as well. Interestingly enough, rushing wind also may symbolize an agitated state of mind in which the unconscious is about to prevail over conscious attitudes and reject empirical conditions and the demands of the workaday world. Certainly the storm of wind and water that Poe describes takes on cosmic dimension with both elements proclaiming their rage, their dissatisfaction with things as they are and their intention to sweep them asunder, as in the biblical flood.

Such upheavals agitate and torment those within their range. The surviving brother, who has tied himself to a water cask and cast himself into the sea, watches his two brothers capsize and sink beneath the waves, holding fast to the ring bolt of the ship.

Psychologically, the tactics of the surviving fisherman are entirely sound. Although he feels the "deadly terror" and "the sickening sweep of the descent," he does not avoid the harrowing experience. That he hurls himself and the barrel to which he is tied into the sea indicates his willingness to undergo whatever ordeal is necessary to gain life, to know the ultimate in catastrophe and terror and to survive.

Never shall I forget the sensation of awe, horror, and admiration with which I gazed about me. The boat appeared to be hanging, as if by magic, midway down, upon the interior surface of a funnel vast in circumference, prodigious in depth, and whose perfectly smooth sides might have been mistaken for ebony, but for the bewildering rapidity with which they spun around, and for the gleaming and ghastly radiance they shot forth, as the rays of the full moon, from that circular rift amid the clouds which I have already described, streamed in a flood of golden glory along the black walls, and far away down into the inmost recesses of the abyss (p. 277).

If an initiation is to be complete, if fresh ideations and attitudes are to prevail, the death experience must at least be acknowledged and the maelstrom traversed; the enormous velocities and heaving waters of the unconscious explored, the vortices, circular configurations, and ensuing sense of disorientation undergone. Such is the all-powerful and redoubtable force that precedes revelation and a theophany. As God questioned Job,

Has thou entered into the springs of the sea? or hast thou walked in the search of the depth? (38:16)
Have the gates of death been opened unto thee? or hast thou seen the doors of the shadow of death? (38:17)

These may be the same questions Poe propounded to himself in his own underworld descents.

The Anima

Poe's creativity was fed by the surgings from the subliminal realm. Once its velocity subsided, a variety of archetypal images became discernible, took on contour and form, and emerged in the written work. Among them are the anima figures portrayed in such tales as "Berenice," "Morella," "Ligeia," "The Fall of the House of Usher," "Eleanora" and symbolically in "The Oval Portrait," "The Black Cat," and "The Sphinx." Each represents a vital part of Poe's psychology and is fascinating to consider in respect to his literary career.

Anima figures have been portrayed in every form and guise from virgin to harlot since time immemorial. They represent Eros—that is, love as passion and the ability to relate to people—and they personify the feminine principle in all her various avatars. Psychologically, the anima may be defined as "an autonomous psychic content in the male personality," a kind of inner woman. As Eros, it is the anima figure that establishes for a man what sort of emotional and sexual relationships he will have with the opposite sex. When a man falls in love, for example, he projects his anima on to an individual woman. If, however, his ego overidentifies with his anima figure, difficulties may well arise; he may be so under the spell of this unconscious force that he is rendered psychologically impotent. When the anima is acknowledged consciously and experienced, it may provide the writer of genius with the deepest and finest kind of human inspiration, like Dante's Beatrice or Petrarch's Laura, those suprapersonal visions who provided their creators with beatific visions and harmony of being.

Poe's anima figures are far from being either glamorous or sexually seductive. "The Morellas and Ligeias," Huysmans wrote, "possessed a vast erudition" and were "deeply imbued with the foggy mists of German metaphysics and the cabalistic mysteries of the ancient East," but they "all had the inert bosoms of boys or angels, all were, so to say, unsexual."[10] Poe's feminine characters are for the most part either disembodied Platonic essences, gentle, young, otherworldly spectral shadows, reincarnated beings, or vampires ready to destroy and dismember the man in highly secret and shrouded ways. They dominate because of the male's sheer weakness and helplessness, his strangely passive condition. In most instances, the narrator displays a longing and need for the feminine principle as well as a fear and hatred of it, indicative of an extreme dependency on the anima.

Each of Poe's nonhuman and half-human anima figures overrides and governs the fate of the male narrator, thus psychologically representing an obsessive fantasy, a distortion of what lay buried deep within his subliminal world. Some of these anima figures are masochists; others are cold, calculating, and enigmatic. Poe's feminine characters for the most part exist only to fill a need in the narrator's psyche. They are not full-fledged beings in their own right, but rather they are beclouded visions, hypnagogic images emerging from some dark, eerie corner of a shadowy world, nocturnal emanations, terrors in the night, revenants (returning spirits), fleeting memories arising from some nearby tomb or sepulcher, thoughts or feelings personified in spectral form. The setting from which these feminine apparitions emanate is usually hostile and mephitic.

If their creator's extraordinary artistry were removed from these tales, they might well be studied as incorporating a series of clinical cases, perhaps inspired or taken directly from medical files. Indeed, Poe kept very much abreast of the scientific research then being done both in Europe and in the United States on personality disorders. He read widely on such subjects as phrenology, mesmerism, and the treatment of the insane as well as on the metaphysical material in vogue at the time. In many of his tales there are incredibly accurate descriptions of illnesses and also allusions to preternatural sicknesses, not physically treatable but of an obsessional or phobic kind.

Poe was particularly drawn to those neurological

indispositions which today are classified as psychogenic. He was also fascinated by hypnosis, then
known as mesmerism.[11] This science allowed the
practitioner to penetrate the patient's inner world
while the patient was asleep, to remove the veil of
conventionality, the masks people don to hide their
private thoughts and feelings. For Poe, psychology
and parapsychological investigations of all types
were a source of discovery; as such, they enhanced
his life and art.

Poe's anima-oriented tales, however, always
explore the pathological and physical disorders
within a philosophical and metaphysical context. His
male narrators are for the most part solitary and introverted, alienated from both the outside world and
themselves. His anima characters hover about, almost imperceptibly at times, against a backdrop of
dim haunting lights or glimmering candles in a
quasi-rarefied atmosphere. They are subpersonali-
ties, incorporeal figments severed from the psyche
as a whole. Each anima figure rules and is ruled by
the narrator. It is he who unravels or unveils the
feelings, memories, perturbations, and associations
of these autonomous apparitions who materialize
and are brought to life for the reader, only to vanish
into oblivion.

"Berenice" (1835)

Berenice is described as the "graceful and energetic" cousin of the "gloomy" and "ill" narrator
Egaeus, the last descendant of an ancient family of
visionaries. (Onomastically, Egaeus may be identified with Aegeus, Theseus's father, who cast himself into the sea and drowned when he thought his
son had been killed by the Minotaur.) Egaeus, who

lives in his ancestral home, spends his days in reading and reveries, continuing the life he has led ever since he was a boy. In time, his intellect so ruled his world that he became what could be alluded to as overly cerebral: he was no longer receiving the nutrients necessary to nourish his body, to maintain some semblance of equilibrium and health. Earth, the visceral and instinctual sphere, has been cut off, with the result that he is "buried in gloom," a condition that soon worsens. Egaeus describes himself as suffering from a morbid disease which has been diagnosed as "monomania" and consisted of mental irritability. For no apparent reason, he spends hours on end focusing on some specific physical object or device: a shadow, a phrase, a thought, whatever comes into his mind. Meditation and introversion such as Egaeus describes may be essential to the study of self, but in his case, they are pushed to the extreme. Since his inner explorations were uncontrolled, the narrator gained no insight into his ailment, which grows steadily worse. Autosuggestion, which Egaeus attempts and which some doctors practiced at this time, was a mental cure and is believed to have been a precursor to psychoanalysis. In Egaeus's case, however, nothing seemed to help.

Egaeus not only cannot conduct his autohypnosis, he cannot even control his condition. He enters into what may be called trances for unknown reasons, driven by some mysterious force. His life was bearable until he and Berenice decided to get married. Then his sickness reached dangerous proportions. A similar transformation occurred in Berenice. Delightful and healthy at the outset of the tale, she now begins to waste away.

Egaeus may be classified as a thinking type; his life is exclusively focused on cerebral speculation, and his existence as a whole is centered on mental ideas, rigid formulae, and values. "Feeling with me," as he himself states, *"had never been* of the heart, and my passions *always were* of the mind." He does not conceive of Berenice as a "living and breathing" being but as the Berenice of a dream—not as a being of the earth, earthly, but as the abstraction of such a being—not as a thing to admire, but to analyze—not as an object of love, but as the theme of the most abstruse although desultory speculation.

Marriage, he thought, might change the relationship, yet Egaeus was well aware of the trauma in store for him. He now "shuddered in her presence, and grew pale at her approach." An adolescent, he unconsciously realized that in no way could he fulfill his role as husband or future father; nor could he give up completely his thinking world by assuming the responsibilities and values of an earthly sphere which would have been his lot as a husband. He has been severed from reality, living as he does in the ancestral past of his fathers, so much so that any sort of actual working relationship with another human being is out of the question. To a certain degree Egaeus's "monomaniac character" represents his way of withdrawing from life, his death wish. Certainly, it is indicative of a schizophrenic state in which fantasy and reality become interchangeable.[12]

Since Berenice is only a projection, she must wait upon the narrator if she is to fulfill herself as wife and mother. She is a kind of spirit, an intangible psychic phenomenon, a split-off from the dissociated psychic content existing in Egaeus's unconscious. Once marriage was decided upon, this *anima rationalis*, or soul image, grew increasingly wan, nervous, and faded, though these symptoms had manifested themselves prior to his marriage proposal. Berenice's nervousness became more and more pronounced because she was no longer being nourished or sustained by Egaeus, who by this time was too involved in his own subliminal sphere to be accessible to anyone. The projection, which had brought her to life in the first place, was slowly diminishing in power and import, indicating the time to be ripe for Berenice's death.

One winter afternoon as Berenice stands silently before Egaeus, an "icy chill" runs through his frame. He observes her "hollow temples, " her high forehead, her very pale yet "singularly placid" face, and most particularly, her "lifeless, and lustreless, and seemingly pupil-less" eyes. He shrinks from "their glassy stare." She was sleepwalking, he reasoned. Then, one image superseded all others in his mind: her teeth, "long, narrow, and excessively white, with pale lips writhing about them."

Two days later, still meditating on "the *phantasma* of the teeth," he hears "troubled voices" outside his room and then screams of dismay. He is informed of Berenice's passing. The burial takes place later. Egaeus returns to his library and must have gone to sleep and dreamed. He feels confused on awakening. A servant enters and tells him that Berenice's grave has been violated, her body disfigured and that a scream had been heard from that area. When the servants went to investigate, they saw her "still breathing, still palpitating, still *alive!*" Then he points to Egaeus's clothes, blood-stained and muddy, and to the spade leaning against the wall. A strange box has been placed next to Egaeus's lamp; he rushes toward it and drops it by mistake. Its contents, now visible, are Berenice's exquisite teeth, along with the dental instruments used to extract them.

Teeth have always been equated with aggression; they fulfill a need by taking from the outer world, cutting, dismembering, and pulverizing in order to nourish soma and psyche. Egaeus longed for them to such an extent that they became the subject of his unconscious meditations, indicating his need for just such a force, one that would be strong enough to extract him from his lethargy. A psychologically castrated being, Egaeus can function only in the enclosed, cell-like construct of his intellect. Teeth represent activity and power, and for this reason primitive people use them as adornments and fetishes. Egaeus seeks to do likewise: to take the teeth for himself so as to be endowed with those elements he lacks: strength and courage. Teeth also indicate sexual energy, of which he is completely devoid, and here too they could remedy what is nonexistent in him. Let us recall the importance of teeth in the world of vampires; they nourished Dracula and his entombed cohorts with the blood of life. So, too, with teeth Egaeus would have the instruments that would enable him to get the food to sustain body and intellect.

The voices Egaeus hears during his trancelike meditation may be considered personifications of unconscious contents, personalities appearing at strange and unexpected moments either enacting what the narrator most needs to know at this particular juncture or revealing insights into the general state of affairs. They are, writes C. G. Jung, comparable to "new character formations," or attempts of the future personality to break through the impasse reached during periods of intense difficulty or psychopathic indispositions.[13] Such is Egaeus's case. He cannot handle the thought of marriage and resents the very idea of altering his life-style.

What the narrator most needed was to strengthen his ego, the center of consciousness, the part of his psyche that related and adapted to both external and inner reality. His ego was functionless, perhaps because of his overemphasis on thinking matters, on the patriarchal past. The thought of having to relate to a woman, to a wife, and to society in general causes him to regress further into a world of his own invention. Such a withdrawal precludes the possibility of any future adaptation. The fact that the narrator does not realize what he has done suggests that he is no longer responsible for his actions. With the disintegration of his personality comes but a single awareness: His salvation lies in the symbolic power of Berenice's teeth, which represent a hierophany for him. His monomania guides him completely.

Violently, brutally, he desecrates her corpse in her grave in order to arrogate to himself what he most needs. He knows no other way since he has never learned to handle the feeling aspects of this personality as represented in Berenice as the anima figure—his feminine side—which has been progressively smothered by the hold of the thinking function, the world of the fathers, the world of books.

"Morella" (1835)

Morella represents to her husband, the narrator, pure intellect, the learning, reasoning function. A beautiful, brilliant woman, she instructs him in the ins and outs of Greek, German, and English philosophy. She symbolizes knowledge incarnate and is a kind of Sophia figure: the highest embodiment of divine feminine wisdom and spiritual love. For her husband she is that force which elevates the reasoning mind above the mundane physical plane with its sordid earthly discords and conflicts. She is purity, abstraction, a crystallization of celestial forces, supernal illumination.

The discussions between husband and wife often center around Friedrich Wilhelm Schelling, who believed in the unity of mind—that is, spirit—and matter. Nature and mind, body and soul, organic and inorganic entities differ only in the degree or level of their development; both eventually will be absorbed, as will all else, into the absolute, the world soul. Schelling wrote: "Nature is visible Spirit, Spirit is invisible Nature."[14] The sense of the unity of all being and of attunement with the cosmos can be experienced through analogy and symbol; it is through these devices that we are able to participate in the vast cosmic flow.

In *Eureka*, Poe summed up his idea on the question of personal identity, termed by him the *principium individuationis* (the principle of becoming individuality), which may or may not be lost at death and which is the preoccupation of both Morella and the narrator, as follows:

The pain of the consideration that we shall lose our identity, ceases at once when we further reflect that the process ... neither more nor less than that of the absorption, by each individual intelligence, of all other intelligences (that is, of the Universe) into its own. That God may be all in all, each must become God (p. 309).

Mysticism divests the individual of uniqueness, transmuting the personal and particular into the spaceless sphere of cosmic consciousness. The same reasoning may be applied to Poe's protagonists. Just as marriage had been the point of rupture between the narrator and Berenice, so the question of individual and independent wills may be said to be the point at which the marital relationship between Morella and her husband begins to founder. The more they delve into occult phenomena, the more the will or nonwill is focused upon, the greater becomes the gulf between the narrator and Morella. She begins to make him feel more and more stifled; unconsciously he longs for her death. (The word "morel" is the name of an edible mushroom, the black nightshade, a parasite.) Although Morella has expanded her husband's horizons, opening his mind up to all kinds of metaphysical and parapsychological ideas, by the same token she has prevented any real development in the other sides of his personality, castrating him psychologically by her single-minded drive to study and learn more. Only when the question of personal identity, of individuality—interpreted as living independent spirit—is probed does he dimly realize that his is slowly smothering. Survival requires that he divest himself of Morella.

The narrator alludes to his wife's hands as "cold." Hands are vehicles which human beings use to relate to the outside world; like teeth, they are aggressive instruments that grab, form, and relate to exterior domains. That they are described as icy indicates their inability to love and to warm the sensate world. Her hands were cold and dead; nothing but the cortex of her brain was active. Even her voice, so beautiful and melodious at the outset of their relationship, was "tainted with terror." Joy vanished; and "the most beautiful became the most hideous."

As the narrator in "Berenice" strangled his body by depriving it of earth and water—organic nourishment—so too will Morella's existence crumble and wither. In time she informs her husband of her pregnancy but also tells him that she will die in childbirth. This occurs. A daughter is born, as beautiful as the mother. As the child grows, she takes on her mother's personality and intelligence. At the age of ten, her father decides to have her baptized. At the font, he hesitates before giving her a Christian

name. Suddenly, some mysterious force impels him
to whisper the name "Morella," to which the child
replies, "I am here!" She falls to the floor and dies.
When the narrator buries his daughter in the family
tomb, he finds no trace of the first Morella.

That the narrator's daughter dies is inevitable.
She is a replica of the mother, who was herself a
projection of the narrator's unconscious, a more ma-
ture aspect of the feminine image. The daughter was
a young girl anima and so must succumb to the same
fate. One fascinating aspect in terms of numerology
is that the narrator should have waited until the girl
was ten years old before having her baptized. To
Pythagoras and his followers, the number ten represents the totality of the universe, the notion of
perfection or completion found in the Tetractys, a
triangle made up of four, three, two, one sections,
all of which add up to ten. At the age of ten, the
second Morella (the narrator's daughter) seemed to
have reached a state of earthly perfection; she could
no longer evolve, only regress, and therefore it is
the moment for her to die, to return to the earth
mother, the archetypal suprapersonal image. Death
is the forerunner of rebirth.

Both Berenice and Morella are relatively
healthy anima figures at the outset of these tales. It
is only when Berenice reaches marriageable age and
would then have to move beyond her innocent gir-
lishness and assume the role of woman that such an
eventuality becomes unacceptable. Then the projection is withdrawn, slowly and in a direct relationship with the march of her disease. When it van-
ishes completely, she does too. The same situation
holds true of Morella, the imbalance here residing
in the notion of independence and individuality.
When the narrator becomes aware of his emotional

impotence and dependence, he no longer can sustain a relationship with this powerful anima figure who dominates his life. For him a rectification is needed; she expires and is re-created in the figure of her daughter. Rather than altering the relationship, fleshing it out, and balancing it with a condition of mutual independence and respect, the domineering female principle is reborn, and the narrator remains unfulfilled.

"Ligeia" (1838)

The Lady Ligeia is an even more strange and phantomesque being than Berenice and Morella, her two direct precursors. Here again, the name "Ligeia" is symbolically evocative. The word comes from the Latin *ligo*, meaning "to bind" or "to tie," and is also reminiscent of the nymph Ligea in Virgil's *Georgics*.

The narrator describes Ligeia as so remote a figure, so distant in all ways that he no longer recalls when and where he first met her, probably somewhere near the banks of the Rhine River, he thinks. Beautiful and captivating, she spoke in a low passionate voice. Her hair was raven black, and so were her eyes. Highly learned, she was "buried in studies of a nature more than all else adapted to deaden impressions of the outward world." She is further described as being so light-footed that she "came and departed like a shadow." She was also ethereal in form, so disembodied in spirit that the narrator confesses that at times he was quite unaware of her presence. Like some figure in an "opium-dream," like "an airy and spirit-lifting vision," she seems to have been a phantasm in the narrator's life, the concretization of an unconscious image. Although he reacted potently to the "dear music of her low sweet voice," he also notes the cold touch of "her marble hand."

Like Berenice before her, Ligeia was doomed from the start to sicken and die. "Man doth not yield him to the angels, *nor unto death utterly*, save only through the weakness of his feeble will" are her last impassioned words to the narrator.

Bereft and solitary, the narrator roams aimlessly about, eventually settling in a remote abbey in England. There he takes a new wife, the fair-haired, blue-eyed Lady Rowena. Their bridal chamber, situated high in a turret, is described as pentagonal in shape, with a vast Venetian glass window of leaden hue and strange and mysterious heavy gold and black tapestries. In this claustrophobic, gloomy atmosphere, Rowena becomes ill; she complains of hearing strange sounds and of unexplained movements. The narrator sits beside her while she dies, and not long before that final end, he suddenly feels some kind of invisible force flutter past him; he sees a shadow upon the carpet and imagines that he hears faint footsteps. The night after Rowena's death, the narrator is again seated by the bed on which her corpse is laid, when a gentle sob disturbs the reverie into which he has sunk. He stares at the corpse of Rowena. The body no longer lies still; it stirs and sobs, and color is visible on the cheeks. Paralyzed with terror, the narrator sees the very body itself being transformed. The fair hair turns to raven black, and as the once blue eyes slowly open, he sees the dark gaze of the Lady Ligeia.

Although Ligeia at the outset of the story is described as being beautiful and captivating, and like her anima predecessors intellectually gifted, she is also portrayed as a shadowy apparition, a kind of mirage, a disembodied spirit, an abstract entity. It

is her eyes that principally differentiate her from
Berenice and Morella. They are "far larger than the
ordinary eyes of our race," the narrator declares, and
seem to belong "above or apart from earth," resembling "the beauty of the fabulous Houri" (Muslim
damsels who were companions promised to the
faithful in paradise). The strange light in them, their
color and brilliance, are beyond human understanding; they are "divine orbs," shining like constella-
tions, reminiscent of Leda's two children, Apollo and
Diana. That the narrator equates Ligeia's eyes with
the stars and planets, removing them from an earthly
human context and placing them in the heavenly
realm, is an expression of his own unfathomable
needs and desires.

Ligeia's eyes are mirrors of her soul. They are
sources of reflected light for the narrator; they stand
for spiritual wisdom and sacred intelligence, as they
had for the ancient Egyptians. Unlike the narrators
in "Berenice" and "Morella," Ligeia's husband is
not always passive. He is curious, wanting to know
more about his wife so as to be able to discern the
message behind those eyes, to understand their
expression, "the many incomprehensible anomalies
of the science of the mind." But each time he thinks
he is on the verge of discovering a burning secret,
of recalling some vanished mystery, the answer
evades him.

The narrator also lacks a strongly structured ego.
He succumbs to Ligeia's "gigantic volition" of the
will that never breaks, a force that dominates all of
life; he yields to her "fierce energy" and "infinite
supremacy." He frequently looks at her with "child-
like confidence," agreeing always to her role as
spiritual guide in their exploration of the occult
worlds. The narrator is clearly a perpetual adolescent, and as Ligeia's power over him grows and her

bonds seem to confine him more concretely, her once-radiant eyes grow dull, "duller than Saturnian lead." It is interesting to note that lead, rhyming with "dead," is a word that Poe uses in his tales over and over again. Equated with the planet Saturn, lead was considered by alchemists the basest of all metals, representing the dark and heavy aspects of existence. As leaden tones were increasingly identified with Ligeia, so her flamboyant intelligence grew wan and ill, and it is no wonder that she died.

Lady Rowena, however, fares no better. The chamber to which she is brought in England abounds in grotesque, lugubrious objects and in leaden tones, "tinted of a leaden hue." Unlike the ancient caves in Egypt and Greece where initiates used to come to experience their death and rebirth rituals in the darkness of the earth, Poe's chamber with its subterranean lighting is a mephitic realm that precludes all healthy growth and renewal.[15] Lead is a poison; it kills anyone exposed to its powers for long periods of time. The vision of Ligeia that appears at the conclusion of the tale may be considered a hallucination, the only form of life that can live and move about in this restricted airless, sunless, and sealed region.

"Ligeia" is a masterpiece in its restrained, but dramatic suspense; it was Poe's avowed favorite.

"The Fall of the House of Usher" (1839)

"The Fall of the House of Usher" is acknowledged to be one of Poe's great works. It was acclaimed by such contemporaries as Baudelaire, Huysmans, Mallarmé, and Barbey d'Aurevilly.

None of Poe's protagonists in these tales of hallucination and death seems able either to understand or to come to grips with his anima figure. Childish in their attitude, lopsided in personality, dependent on their own projections of the feminine principle to carry them through life, they are cut off and isolated from the world. In "The Fall of the House of Usher," the reader immediately is immersed in an oppressive leaden atmosphere. The entire opening scene is steeped in blackness and melancholy. "The depressing influence of fear," Huysmans suggested, "acting on the will, like those anaesthetics that paralyze sensibility and that curare that annihilates the nervous elements of motion," have taken over.[16] Ruin and death permeate the atmosphere and proceedings.

When the narrator who is coming to stay with his boyhood friend Roderick Usher, the owner of a large ancestral estate, crosses the causeway to approach the house, he sees the reflection of the vast decaying old mansion in the "featureless tarn" before him. Looking up at the huge gloomy edifice, he notices that there is a "fissure" in the wall extending from the roof line to the bottom of the building. Once he makes his way into the somber, labyrinthian complex, he is struck by the decrepit antique furniture and worn, faded tapestries. Even greater dismay overtakes him when he sees his friend's "cadaverous" eyes, "large, liquid and luminous beyond comparison." The narrator further notes that his friend's lips are very thin and "very pallid." Roderick Usher explains that he suffers from a strange nervous disease which makes him sensitive to "a host of unnatural sensations."

He suffered much from a morbid acuteness of the senses; the most insipid food was alone endurable; he could wear only garments of a certain texture; the odors of all flowers were oppressive; his eyes were tortured by even a faint light; and there were but peculiar sounds, and those from stringed instruments, which did not inspire him with horror (p. 202).

Usher's disease may be clinically authenticated. A case in point is that of Gustav T. Fechner (1801–87), a German minister and experimental physicist who underwent an emotional collapse. His sickness was diagnosed as a neurotic depression with hypochondriacal symptoms complicated by a lesion of the retina. During his illness Fechner lived in isolation in a darkened room; even the walls were painted black. He was unable to tolerate most foods and had reached an almost life-death condition, when by some strange occurrence, a friend of the family had a dream in which she was told how and what to feed Fechner. His improvement progressed from that time on, and he was able to continue his active life. He did, however, change his profession from physicist to natural philosopher.[17]

Madeline Usher, Roderick's sister, is given to trances and sleepwalking and is completely unaware of the world surrounding her, even of the visitor's presence in the family home. That Poe was fascinated by hypnotic trances is not surprising. During the eighteenth and nineteenth centuries, "magnetic sleep," as hypnotic trances were called, were the subject of considerable medical research, along with hysterical and catatonic cataleptic states.[18] According to certain physicians, during periods of catalepsy, the brain was considered to be an instrument of increased perception and sensibility, more acute than during the waking state. It was looked upon as a kind of adapter, a transmitter to be tapped so as to reveal information which could not be known otherwise. Father Faria, for example, who claimed to have studied in India, gave a course on posthypnotic suggestion in Paris in 1812.[19] Philosophers such as

Schelling and Schubert also were fascinated by the mysteries of subliminal spheres, and they believed in the prophetic capacities of these regions. Writers such as Clemens Brentano wrote about specific cases, including that of Katharina Emmerich, a young peasant from Westphalia who bore the stigmata of Christ's passion during her cataleptic states. For two years Brentano went to see her every morning and noted down her statements. His book *Nach den Betrachtungen der gottseligen Anna Katharina Emmerich* resulted from this research.[19]

Madeline Usher's cataleptic condition affects Roderick Usher deeply. He sees her wandering about the house, her physical being eroding daily, but he does nothing about it. It is she who is the anima figure, who has been Roderick's sole companion for many years and he has kept himself within this orbit—the family compound, a psychologically incestuous relationship. She is the force that attaches him still further to what he calls his "race," his home, and his unconscious fantasy image. Roderick's inner state has grown increasingly isolated.

Roderick Usher spends his days reading, delving into alchemical tracts and occult works of all types, and dwelling upon macabre images from the past. One evening he recites a poem, "The Haunted Palace," in which he compares the disintegration of the human personality to a "tottering" building with "lofty reason" placed on the throne of an unstable, decrepit edifice.

Some few days later, he announces that his sister, Madeline, has died. He has decided, however, to keep her coffined body for a fortnight in an iron-clad vault before interring the corpse in the somewhat remote family burial ground. He asks his friend to assist him in carrying out his plan. The narrator agrees and thus comes to see clearly Madeline's face for the first time. She is her brother's duplicate, his identical twin.

Poe's descriptions at this point abound in vegetative imagery: fungi, rotting plants, trees, moldy stones, etc. Vegetative imagery is used frequently in literary works to delineate a comatose or senile condition. Since vegetation feeds directly on inorganic matter, it is looked upon as being connected with the chemical somatic process. To express this condition, Poe introduces plant life in its most rudimentary and negative form, underscoring the miasmic elements in the tale.

Time passes and then one night, during a huge and terrifying storm, clanging, clanking sounds are heard echoing through the maze of corridors in the Usher mansion. Roderick shudders and then shrieks that it is his sister. She is not dead; they have buried her alive. The door swings open, and the ghastly apparition of Madeline in her death agony stands before the two men.

There was blood upon her white robes, and the evidence of some bitter struggle upon every portion of her emaciated frame. For a moment she remained trembling and reeling to and fro upon the threshold, then, with a low moaning cry, fell heavily inward upon the person of her brother, and in her violent and now final death-agonies, bore him to the floor a corpse, and a victim to the terrors he had anticipated (p. 211).

Like an ancient initiate sequestered underground to pray in a deep vault or cave until the moment of rebirth comes to pass, Madeline emerges from the recesses of the darkened underworld. Unlike the practitioner of an ancient mystery religion, however, she comes from her interrred casket to seek vengeance on her brother, who sought to rid himself of her, to entomb her prematurely. She refuses to be swallowed up by the earth alone and demands that her brother share in this last and final transformation. Forcing herself upon Roderick, she puts an end to his passive, listless, lethargic existence as well as to her own.

It is Madeline, the anima figure, who takes the initiative and brings to an end the negative and destructive relationship. The twin beings who issued from a single egg are to return to the *prima materia* as one. Unable to grow in light, too ill to encounter the outside world, brother and sister were thrust upon themselves to live out a stunted, disintegrating existence that could never evolve.

After the death of the brother and sister, the narrator precipitately flees. As he crosses the causeway, he sees by the light of the blood-red moon the fissure in the wall of the house suddenly widen and the whole vast building crumble and fall into the dark waters of the tarn. In the same way that the image had arisen as a phantasm, an afterdream common, Poe tells us, to "the reveller of opium," so it must again sink back into the submerged subliminal spheres, there to remain.

"Eleanora" (1842)

In "Eleanora" the reader encounters the first positive anima figure created by Poe. Autobiographically, this tale is almost prophetic in its vision, for Poe wrote and published it the year before Virginia's first hemorrhage.

All through their childhood and youth, the narrator, who is five years older than his cousin Eleanora, live with her mother in the idyllic seclusion of the Valley of the Many-Colored Grass, with its fragrant flowers, its trees of bright green foliage, and its crystalline river, which seems an earthly paradise. When the two young people grow up and fall in love, however, the surroundings gradually begin to change: The grass deepens its hue, brilliant red flowers spring up, and the river fills with gold and silver fish. All nature seems to be burgeoning with intensified life and beauty. New life and growth also imply decline, however; intimations of death are felt as the boy and girl move from childhood to early adolescence and then to sexual maturity.

When Eleanora broaches the subject of her imminent death, and with it, her departure from this ideal land, the narrator promises that should she indeed die, he will continue to live on in the valley. True to his word, after Eleanora's death he stays in the valley. In time, however, the place becomes increasingly lonely. He longs to experience another love, to replace his loss. He leaves to take up life at court in a foreign city, and there he falls in love with Ermengarde, whom he marries. Although he has broken his vow, he does not feel guilt-ridden, for Eleanora's voice, sighing in the wind, comes to him, absolving him. In heaven, all will be explained and forgiven, she whispers to him.

Psychologically, the Edenlike atmosphere that the narrator and Eleanora shared is comparable to the world of the child or the adolescent before the awakening of consciousness. Only when recognition of life's duality exists, of its essential polarities— birth and death, day and night, masculine and feminine—can one begin to experience individuality and a sense of one's own personal worth and being. That is the point, too, when one becomes free from a passive acceptance of the inherited parental world of nature.

Eleanora and the narrator lived as twin egos, similar in some respects to Roderick and Madeline

Usher, except that their lives were idyllic. Eleanora's death represents the suppression and disappearance of the young anima figure who cannot be permitted to enter into maturity and motherhood and cannot assume the responsibilities and difficulties of adult life. Unlike Psyche and Persephone, who experienced the trials and tribulations that go hand in hand with the maturation process, Eleanora disappears forever from the narrator's sight to exist spirtually as a whispering voice in the wind. Devoid of corporeal temporality, transmuted into a spiritual force that lives only within the masculine psyche, she will continue to watch over the spirit of her beloved.

That the narrator chooses to fill the void in his life with the love of another woman is healthy and natural. By so doing, he casts his vote for growth and life, willing to break his promise and thus violate whatever internal prohibitions previously impelled his development. In fact, it is because he is unafraid, since he has never been exposed to guilt or fear, that he is able to do so, and he continues to live in a virtually similar sphere. Guilt takes on meaning only with objective vision, with consciousness and conscience. When the whispering voice of Eleanora tells him that all will be explained in heaven, he remains unscathed but also unchanged. To escape the consequences of one's behavior, as the narrator, thanks to the supernatural intervention of Eleanora, is able to do, is to reject responsibility for one's behavior and actions.

Eleanora and Ermengarde are both personifications of the anima archetype: the young girl or virgin, and the hetaira or sexually seductive woman. Both of them influence and foster the narrator's desire, and either of them might have led to his development but did not.

As in much romantic literature, where the supernatural predominates and mystical oneness is the goal of the protagonist, Poe also feels deeply for and with nature, as opposed to what he sometimes refers to as the dry, arid, and overly rational outlook of the Age of Enlightenment. Like the romantics, too, his anima figures are immersed in ideal and protective realms, where, as in this tale, the natural world is arrayed in its most beautiful and sparkling guise and life is apparently a wholly harmonious and happy state. Cradled in this paradisial yet parasitic and sheltered existence, his anima figures are freed from any sense of or need for adult responsibility. Poe's narrators as well feel little connection with the outside world and lead a life devoid of antagonism and conflict, simply because the dichotomies existent in the actual world are unknown to them.[20]

"The Oval Portrait" (1842)

"The Oval Portrait" takes the reader ever more deeply into the realm of the supernatural. Reminiscent of Balzac's tales "The Red Inn" and "The Unknown Masterpiece" and Nerval's "The Devil's Portrait," Gautier's "Arria Marcella," and Hawthorne's "The Birthmark," Poe brings to life yet another gentle, yielding anima figure who is doomed to die.

A young man who has been sorely wounded and his servant take shelter for the night in an empty château in the Appenines, a gloomy enclave which, as the narrator suggests, Mrs. Radcliffe might well have used as the setting of one of her terrifying Gothic tales. The young man selects for his quarters a room in one of "the least sumptuously furnished apartments" in a remote turret of the vast edifice. Knowing that he will be unable to sleep, he tells his servant not to close the black curtains encircling the bed and to leave the candelabrum lit. He plans to spend the night reading a book that is on the table beside the bed, describing the paintings on the walls of the room he occupies.

At midnight, he moves the position of the candelabrum on the table beside him in order to see better, and as he does so, one of the paintings hanging on the wall in a niche suddenly becomes visible. He sees the portrait of a young girl just "ripening into womanhood" in a richly wrought, gold oval frame. The narrator immediately shuts his eyes and even as he does so, wonders why he had so acted. "To gain time for thought," to make sure that his vision has not deceived him, he reasons. Almost instantly he reopens his eyes, and "half sitting, half reclining," he gazes at the portrait for nearly an hour. He finds himself increasingly captivated by the girl's absolute "life-likeness of expression." Becoming more and more agitated, he again changes the position of the candelabrum, and the painting becomes shrouded in darkness. He resumes his reading, turning to the place in the volume that describes the painting which so fascinates him. He learns that the remarkable likeness of the girl had been painted by her husband. She was very much in love with the artist husband and he with her, but as she sat for him and he worked on the portrait day after day and week after week, he became so engrossed in his painting that he failed to realize that her health was steadily failing. And she, for her part, was unwilling to disturb the pleasure he took in his work. At last the portrait was completed to his satisfaction. Exclaiming, "This is indeed *Life itself*!" he turned to look at his beloved wife only to find her dead.

This story of Poe's bears a marked resemblance to that of Eleanora, the maiden who could not live

on as wife. The day the beautiful girl depicted in
"The Oval Portrait" married her artist husband,
"evil" descended upon her. "Art was her rival," Poe
wrote, because art has the power to arrest the flux
of time and eternalize the transient. Reflecting perhaps his underlying fear of the marital experience,
her artist husband removed all possibility of change
and in so doing killed the active, ever-changing cycle
of birth, growth, maturity, old age, death and rebirth
that all those who would participate in life's eternal
round must learn to accept. It is only the work of
art that as long as it exists will remain forever.

"The Black Cat" (1843)

"The Black Cat" is one of Poe's most famous and
also most terrifying tales, and it reveals the narrator's
inability to cope with his marriage to an older woman. He is quick to confess that he has undergone a
personality change. In his youth he was humane and
fond of pets, and at the beginning of his marriage
he and his wife acquired a cat named Pluto, whom
they both loved. Perhaps what occurred would not
have happened if he had not begun to drink. In any
case, he progressively becomes more and more peev-
ish, moody, and short-tempered. One night, as he
is returning home intoxicated, it seems to him that
Pluto is avoiding him. He is so outraged by the
thought that he seizes the cat and with his penknife
cuts out one of its eyes. He is horrified at first by
his hideous deed, but his guilt and horror turn before
long into resentful anger. The cat understandably
begins avoiding him, and so one night the narrator
in a perverse rage again seizes the cat and this time
kills him by making a noose and taking the beast
outside the house to hang it from a tree. Later that

night the narrator's home is destroyed by fire. Only
the wall remains standing. He and his wife find
quarters in an old dilapidated building. One evening, while drinking in the local saloon, he becomes
attracted to a huge one-eyed cat seated on a cask of
rum. Since no one claims the animal, he takes it
home with him. The cat is greatly taken by the narrator's caresses and in time becomes fond of his wife
too. Perhaps for this reason, the narrator finds himself increasingly irked by the beast, jealous of the
animal's affection for his wife. Furthermore, he notices that what had been merely a white splotch on
the cat's chest has now taken on the markings and
shape of a gallows. One day, as he and his wife go
down to the cellar and the cat follows, he decides
in a sudden rage to do away with the animal. Seizing
an ax and raising it to slaughter the cat, he instead
kills his wife, who had attempted to prevent the action. Coolly and methodically he places her lifeless
body in a recess in the cellar wall, which he then
bricks over. And the cat—he is greatly relieved to
find—has disappeared.

Four days later, the police arrive to investigate
what they have been told is the disappearance of a
woman. The narrator satisfies them that nothing is
amiss, and they are about to leave, when he delays
their departure. He evidently wants to be found out.
He remarks on the solidity of the cellar wall, which
he then takes them down to see. He even pounds
on the wall behind which his wife's corpse is incarcerated. Suddenly an unearthly sobbing is heard.
The police break down the wall; and on the head
of a "greatly decayed" corpse "clotted with gore,"
sits the cat "with red extended mouth and solitary
eye of fire."

The cat, which symbolizes the anima figure in
Poe's tale, was associated in ancient Egypt with Isis,

identified so frequently with the moon. Ironically, in the light of Poe's tale, the cat was once considered to be the guardian of marriage, but it is also identified with witches and with death sorcery and darkness. In Kabbalistic and Buddhist belief, the cat frequently is associated with the serpent, indicating its sinuous and sometimes treacherous nature and also its wise, secretive, and mysterious manner. Arcane and sometimes almost preternaturally clever in its ways, the cat is endowed, some mystics believe, with clairvoyance. For this reason, ancient African medicine bags were made of wild cat skin. It is interesting to note, in this connection, that the cat and the serpent were the only two animals to remain unmoved at the Buddha's death, thus revealing their superiority in that they had reached the stage in spiritual evolution when earthly entanglements are no longer of import, when the transpersonal and eternal take precedence.

In Poe's tale, the narrator considers the two cats obstacles to his happiness. He sees them both as judging and condemning him and what he represents. Unable to relate to their vital animality in any way, particularly when he is drunk, he cuts out the eye of the first, eradicating that instrument of perception which observes him and knows him for what he is: a weakly structured individual who resorts to alcohol in order to anesthetize himself and avoid whatever sexual and marital encounters he might have to face.

Eyes play an important role in other of Poe's anima tales: "Berenice," "Morella," and "Ligeia." As said before, the eye is not only the physical means of perception, it is a mediator between the objective and subjective worlds. Its power, under other circumstances, might have helped the narrator become cognizant of his own limitations and thus acknowl-

edge the difference between what he believes himself to be and what he really is. In so doing, he might
have penetrated into the very heart of the matter—
the source of his anger, his rage, and violence. The
cat's eye is a mirrorlike force which might have allowed him to speculate about the intangible and to
gain a deeper understanding of his own being, but
since he found it impossible to peer into his depths,
he had to get rid of the animal upon which he projected.

In the course of the story, the narrator mentions
that his wife made frequent allusions to the ancient
popular notion that cats are like witches; negative
forces. Poe himself made a similar statement in his
essay, "Instinct vs Reason—a Black Cat," in which
he comments, "Black cats are all of them witches."
Psychologically, witches are materializations of
dreaded forces that exist deep within the unconscious, repressed instincts that wreak terror and
havoc on those who repress them, which is the precise case of Poe's narrator. Usually hideously deformed, witches serve the powers of darkness as opposed to those of light; they represent what is
instinctual, unintegrated, irrational, and therefore
dangerous within the human psyche.

That Poe should have equated the instincts with
a black cat in both his essay and tale is particularly
fascinating in the light of another of his statements:
"Instinct, so far from being inferior to reason, is perhaps the most exalted intellect of all. It will appear
to the true philosopher as the divine mind itself acting *immediately* upon its creatures." Because the
cat in the animal realm represents what Morella,
Berenice, and Ligeia symbolize in the human
sphere, both the animal and the wife had to be done
away with.

The blazing fire that engulfs the house after

Pluto's hanging may represent a kind of purgatorial symbol, an attempt on the part of the narrator to wipe out remorse and whatever pangs of guilt he feels. Ritualistic fire both purifies and destroys, thus permitting new life and growth to begin. Important also is the house imagery, in which the cellar is equated with the unconscious. That the narrator goes down to these lower regions to perform his murderous act indicates the necessity he feels to contact those primitive elements of being, that vegetative domain which played such a powerful role in "The Fall of the House of Usher." The wall into which the narrator bricked up his wife's body is indeed his way of shutting away what the feminine principle represents, imprisoning it so that it will never become a threat to him. That at the end he sees the cat seated on his wife's head is reminiscent of the raven that squats on the bust of Pallas in Poe's poem. It is the intellect, that powerful force, the dominating factor that he most fears. Like Lady Macbeth, the narrator can never wipe this indelible stain away either through repentance, ritualistic washing, or murder.

The narrator's need to have his deed unmasked is as powerful an element within his subliminal realm as his need to extirpate and kill. He understands the potential evil that lies at the core of his personality and wants to stop the further murderous deeds of which he knows he is capable. Like a child who demands chastisement in order to pay for his wrongdoing, the narrator looks for some collective force to imprison his evil nature. It is not surprising that Poe in "Instinct vs Reason" should write:

that the boundary between instinct and reason is of a very shadowy nature. The black cat, in doing what she did, must have made use of all the perceptive and reflective faculties which we are in the habit of supposing the prescriptive qualities of reason alone (p. 359).

"The Sphinx" (1846)

"The Sphinx" is a further exploration into the anima image, but here it is a hallucinatory premonitory force. In this tale, the narrator is visiting a friend in the country in order to escape from a cholera epidemic. He spends much of his time reading from the books in his host's library. One warm afternoon, he happens to look out of the window and in the distance sees an enormous monster with a huge mouth and nose, shaggy hair, tusks, crystal wings, metal scales, and on its breast a death's-head, which he takes as a prophecy of his own approaching demise. A few days later he again sees the monster; this time, however, his host, sitting with him, fails to catch even a glimpse of the dread apparition. The host takes down a scientific book from his shelves and reads a certain passage out loud; it fits the description of the emblem on the so-called monster, inasmuch as it deals with a death's-headed sphinx, a variety of insect. While he is reading the description to his friend, he happens to look at the window in front of him and sees the monstrous insect he had been describing, climb up the side of the window.

The death's-head is, of course, a representation of the human skull and has been the symbol of death and terror throughout the history of the human race. It is also the name of a very large, dark European hawkmoth (*Archerontia atropos*) that bears on the back of its thorax markings highly resembling those of the human skull. According to Poe's tale, it also utters a "melancholy cry," warning of oncoming disaster. That this moth should have been associated with death is therefore entirely understandable. The Aztecs looked upon it as a symbol of the soul, of the last vital breath which escaped from the dying person's mouth.

The moth in Poe's tale is identified with effigies of the sphinx, those prodigious stone constructions built in the desert by the ancient Egyptians, colossal shapes which cast their long shadow before them, guarding and protecting the pyramids under which the royal dead lie buried. A transpersonal force, the Sphinx watched over mummified kings and queens and observed time turning to eternity. The sphinx is basically a feline feminine force; like the cat, its countenance exhibits neither fear nor terror but remains impassive and immobile. Because of its objective and emotionless expression, which Poe also noted on the cat's face in "The Black Cat" and elsewhere, the sphinx is identified with the perversely feminine side of women, as, for example, in the Oedipus myth when the sphinx ravaged entire regions, punishing all those who had unwittingly disobeyed the natural law.[21]

In Poe's tale, the etymology of the genus sphinx of the *Crepuscularia* family, belonging to the Lepidoptera order of insects, is clearly given to increase the scientific authenticity of the tale. The narrator's vision of the monster has a numinous value. It is an archetypal image and therefore charged with the energy and emotional power of a repressed instinct. The narrator has left the outer world to escape the cholera epidemic to find for himself what he considers to be a safe place. This supposedly sheltered, fixed position in which he can reorient himself, he now realizes, is not secure at all. A monstrous force is attempting to destroy him from within, indicating the narrator's own interior fears and apprehension about death.

The archetypal image emerging from his collective unconscious has taken the form of a vast apparition, bearing feline characteristics—a Hecate of sorts—predictive, he believes, of his own death.

The synchronistic happening occurs when the

host takes down the book and reads the description of the real death's-headed sphinx and then sees a living insect of this very kind crawling up the outside of the window. This was not a hallucination but a psychological happening. C. G. Jung later related a similar incident, concerning a scarab:

A young woman I was treating had, at a critical moment, a dream in which she was given a golden scarab. While she was telling me this dream, I sat with my back to the closed window. Suddenly I heard a noise behind me, like a giant tapping. I turned round and saw a flying insect knocking against the window-pane from outside. I opened the window and caught the creature in the air as it flew in. It was the nearest analogy to a golden scarab that one finds in our latitudes, scarabaeid beetle, the common rose-chafer (*cetonia aurata*), Which contrary to its usual habits had evidently felt an urge to get into a dark room at this particular moment.[22]

The death-headed sphinx was an archetypal force that had emerged from the collective unconscious. As the image is given form, a host of hitherto repressed emotions floods the narrator's consciousness.

In Poe's tale, it is this hallucinatory and synchronistic event that warns the narrator that any attempt to withdraw into safety is illusory. The enemy attacks from within; the fear of life and the fear of death are insidious and often one and the same, destroying the individual's already weakly structured ego if not the person's ultimate being.

Nearly all the anima figures in Poe's remarkable tales either waste away and die or are killed. Only in "Eleanora" is the narrator allowed to live on, but as an emotionally stunted individual; and in "The Sphinx," after the discovery of the reality of the psychological danger involved, the protagonist is permitted to leave.

Any change or development between husband

and wife in Poe's tale is also halted; male and female
are unable to advance beyond the adolescent stage,
to assume the responsibilities that the processes of
growth and maturation entail. If forced to progress
into the mainstream of existence, these anima figures
either die or are killed, reappearing to haunt the
narrator's disturbed psyche. Each in her own way
is a projection of the narrator's unconsicous in that
borderline zone in which the real and unreal, life
and death, sanity and madness coexist.

The Shadow

Psychologically, the shadow is composed of those
unconscious characteristics which the conscious
mind has found incompatible and has therefore rejected or repressed. Shadow characteristics frequently are personified in dreams in the guise of
murderers, alcoholics, drug addicts, derelicts, or
other objectionable types, and they are usually of
the same sex as the dreamer. Unless the shadow is
recognized as possessing qualities of one's own personality and unless these characteristics are integrated into the psyche as a whole and not bypassed
or rejected, negative shadow images may become
highly destructive, acting out their own needs in a
deleterious manner. If, on the other hand, those
forces which are thought of as unworthy and negative are understood as part of the whole personality,
they may come to work in a positive personal way.
    In the tales discussed in this section—"William
Wilson," "The Man of the Crowd," "The Masque
of the Red Death," "The Pit and the Pendulum,"
"The Tell-Tale Heart," "The Imp of the Perverse,"
and "The Cask of Amontillado"—the shadow figure
emerges as a personification of the narrator's hostile

feelings and thoughts, symbolizing the repressed instincts of the personality. As these macabre beings live out their earthly peregrinations in the form of ancestral spirits, ghosts, ghouls, murderers, and psychopaths, they appear and disappear, drowning and then bobbing up again during the course of the story, twining themselves about the narrator in parasitic array, each expelling venom and enacting fantasies, perhaps as a ritual defense against an even more hideous fate.

That Poe's tales are replete with shadow personalities may be due to the constricted moral view of life then prevalent which jarred with his own artistic temperament. It is, of course, not only the cultural canon of a society that paves the way for the flourishing of a shadow archetype; that also depends on the individual's own approach to life, which may be compounded by a neurotic or pathological condition. Society demands conscious identification with the dominant, the accepted way. Poe was far from the usual or normal kind of person who blends into society. Orphaned, poor, rejected by the foster father in whom he had longed to put his trust, he found it difficult to reconcile his feelings with the prevailing mores. Nor did his sensitive nature allow him easily to brush off the slights and frequent insults leveled at him. He reacted overtly, angrily at times, and therefore found it difficult to get along with people. He was unable to adapt to the norm, and the more pained he felt, the colder the outside world seemed, and the greater became his solitude. Nevertheless, Poe tried and succeeded in finding his way in the world; although he despised society for inflicting such hardships on him—mostly of an economic nature—he struggled to make a place for himself and to survive. He worked hard, and if this did not always succeed in filling the till, he wrote

to friends for money, hoping for kindness. He lived
modestly and certainly as frugally as possible with
his child bride and her mother. Poe's critical faculties, which his newspaper and editorial functions
sharpened, grew increasingly acute as the years
passed. Sometimes his evaluations of novels, poems,
and essays were cutting and unwarrantingly harsh.
Yet this kind of literary endeavor allowed him to rid
himself of some of the venom that clutched so pain-
fully at his heart. He felt himself striking back, at
those forces in society—or particular individuals—
who might have wronged him.

Resentment and anger also are built into his
tales. His narrators for the most part live introverted
existences, virtually closing the door to health and
well-being. In their secluded and miasmic worlds,
where rage rises and persists, they believe that by
analyzing their feelings, they may gain better insight
into their corrupt souls. What they do achieve is to
explicate for the reader their motivations, to sort out
their reasons for killing and mutilating their enemies, although such enlightenment always comes
after the fact—when it is too late to undo their mis-
deeds. They are thinking beings who dissect their
emotions and ideations but do not acquire sufficient
knowledge to transform their own personalities. The
dichotomy between what the protagonists would
have wanted to be and what they are gives the reader
the impression of being positioned between Scylla
and Charybdis, those six-headed sea monsters ready
to destroy whoever comes within range.

Poe's narrators in this group of tales think and
reason; they dissect their views of their situation.
In so doing, they repress what they feel unworthy
of an admirable being. Their energy, therefore, is
focused inward; all evil characteristics are blocked
inside the psyche, creating extreme tension between

the image the individual has of himself and his real intrinsic nature. Poe might have said of his protagonists the words that Goethe gave to Faust: "Two souls, alas, are housed within my breast."

Although Poe's protagonists question their thoughts and feelings as well as their motivations and analyze the amount of harm they have done, they rarely grow in understanding. They lack the detachment necessary to rectify the situation and the will to carry out their decisions once these are made. Solipsistic in every way, they are caught in the stifling world of their own choice. Frequently they fall victim to the very evil they try to avoid, so mesmerized are they by the transpersonal shadow force inhabiting their psyches and shocked by the depth and range of its propensity for evil. Although they would like to confront the shadow and annul its force, the one-sidedness of their behavior patterns makes for such an imbalance that they are swallowed up by its very power. They even enjoy unconsciously what they consider to be their success in depravity. In "The Black Cat," for example, the narrator longs to be discovered and goes to great lengths to ensure that he will be. In "The Imp of the Perverse," the protagonist feels impelled to confess his ignominious deed. Like the voyeur, he delights in pointing out the aberration of his behavior—its uniqueness— deriving both pleasure and pain in so doing. The punishment exacted by society may serve, psychologically and religiously, to bring him pardon and redemption by ridding him of his guilt, but nothing can alter his passivity. Poe's characters, however, do not usually feel guilt or the need to atone. Punishment rarely alters their psychological makeup. Their turmoil is perpetual, as is the reenactment of their deeds.

The acceptance of one's good and evil charac-

teristics through an act of cognition should expand
consciousness, giving light to what has darkness.
Poe's protagonists, however, remain entrapped in
their circumscribed infernal regions.

"William Wilson" (1839)

"William Wilson," which is a classic of its kind, introduces readers to a double personality, not unlike
that found in E. T. A. Hoffmann's "The Devil's
Elixir," Nerval's *Singular Biography of Raoul Spi-
fame,* or Dostoyevsky's *The Double.* What distin-
guishes Poe's tale from these, however, is that in
"William Wilson," the shadow figure represents
what society considers to be just, upright, and honorable, whereas the narrator's ego (center of the
conscious personality) is looked upon as an imped-
iment, a negative factor that blocks out all his happiness and joy.

As the narrator begins the tale, he announces
that he is approaching death and that his name is
William Wilson. though this is really not his name.
A mystery surrounds him that he must try to unravel.
It is his personality that he does not understand. As
a youngster, his parents doted on him; he was self-
willed and possessed a highly excitable temperament. When he was sent to Reverend Dr. Bransby's
school, modeled after the one Poe attended in England, Wilson had a strange encounter. He met a lad
who had the same name, who entered the school on
the same day he had, who looked like him in every
way. Their relationship was complex, marked with
ambiguities. In time, the "other" imitated him in
his gait, his habits, his manner, even his voice. He
spoke in a "singular whisper" because of a weakness

in the guttural organs. They began quarreling; jealousy set in on the narrator's part.

In time the narrator goes off to Eton. There he is caught up in some brawls and drunken escapades. On one occasion, he suddenly hears the whisper of the "other," which so shocks him that he is made sober instantly. On to Oxford. As the narrator gambles, a cloaked figure enters the scene: a stranger who stands in partial darkness and whispers to those gathered around the gambling table that they should look in the inner linings of William Wilson's sleeve. They find there the cards necessary for the game. The narrator is expelled from Oxford and spends a long period traveling abroad.

In Rome during the carnival season he is about to seduce the wife of a Neapolitan duke, when the "other" again intervenes to right a wrong. This time the narrator is furious and drags what he considers to be the evildoer into an antechamber. He forces him to the floor and then plunges his sword into him "with brute ferocity, repeatedly through and through his bosom." He notices a large mirror at the far end of the room, and as he looks into it, he sees his "own image, but with features all pale and dabbled in blood" advancing toward him. But it really was not he in the mirror. "It was my antagonist—it was Wilson, who then stood before me in the agonies of his dissolution." Speaking "no longer in a whisper," the narrator thought he could have been speaking when he heard: "You have conquered, and I yield. Yet, henceforward art thou also dead—dead to the World, to heaven and to Hope! In me didst thou exist—and, in my death, see by this image, which is thine own, how utterly thou hast murdered thyself."

At the outset of the tale, the narrator comments

on the fact that he had been indulged by his parents and never really knew any form of discipline at home, nor had moral values been inculcated into him. Only in the collective atmosphere of school does he becomes conscious of his upbringing or lack of it; in the organized traditional world of the English public school, directed by a clergyman, he begins to objectify and to think about his situation and his life. Polarities then come into being, and with them, self-knowledge emerges for the narrator. His first encounter with the "other" takes place at school, when his parents no longer are present to coddle him. The double or shadow factor fulfilled a need, in his life. He represses his feelings of anger and jealousy, which by being projected on to the "other" take on such power that the narrator finally considers his rival a threat to his well-being, to that way upon which he seeks to pattern his life-style. The identification has taken on such reality for the narrator that in time he can no longer distinguish the real person from the abstract notion.

After leaving the school the "other" is always there, whenever the narrator seeks to countermand society's dictates. The decisive confrontation takes place in Rome during the carnival season. This is a time for feasting and revelry: just before Lent, the forty days from Ash Wednesday to Easter, observed by fasting and penitence to commemorate Jesus's fasting in the wilderness. It is on this occasion that individuals may lose their inhibitions; it is at this juncture that the narrator will come to terms with his double, that he will take note of what he considers to be his evil self in the mirror at the conclusion of the tale.

Symbolically, mirrors represent consciousness because they reflect the visible world. Yet they are ambiguous since the images contained in a mirror may distort features and pacify the observer. The mirror in many myths and legends represents the door to the unknown, to the land of spirits; it opens onto another existence—from life to death. In Jean Cocteau's *Orpheus*, the personification of death enters the world of the living through the mirror. In Poe's tale, the mirror stands for truth, and the struggle takes place before this symbol, paving the way for the double's entrance into that other world and his death.

Archetypes in general may be glimpsed only when activated. That the narrator's shadow figure came into existence at school is understandable; it grew out of necessity. Alone, without the protective atmosphere of his parental home, the narrator needed some force to replace this loss. The double then appeared; the shadow factor became solidly linked to him, and whenever the narrator acts in what society considers an evil manner, the shadow image is activated and seemingly takes on a life of its own. Only at the end of the tale does the narrator seek to remedy the situation. He will no longer accept the double passively; the disruption caused by him is too great. The question to be posed is the following: Can one annihilate what is so deeply embedded in the psyche? The narrator attempted to do so and believed he had succeeded until he heard a voice— no longer the whisper—say to him: "How utterly thou hast murdered thyself," implying that what he had really murdered was that side of this personality that he could not acknowledge and integrate into consciousness.

In the nineteenth century, shadow characteristics frequently were referred to as other selves and were explored by medical researchers in their quest to understand the subliminal spheres. They were identified with role-playing, regression, hysteria, and neurological disturbances of all kinds, with revealing the patients' latest wishes in certain cases, with a whole hidden domain. The concept of the double ego, or dipsychism as it was called at the time—schizophrenia today—was in the air, and Poe was held spellbound by the coexistence of two such personalities as those of William Wilson and his double, the one adhering to and the other violating society's canon. Under Poe's expert guidance, this story possesses the harrowing lure of terror and the unknown.

"The Man of the Crowd" (1840)

The shadow factor manifests itself in an even stranger fashion in "The Man of the Crowd." The tale takes its readers into terrifying domains of the surreal, worlds in which all seems natural and understandable and yet is not. The shadow in time assumes complete power over the narrator, and only at the end does he realize that there are "secret burdens" that may never be unearthed and accepts the pain involved in the experience of life itself.

The narrator of "The Man of the Crowd," who lives in London, has been kept housebound by illness. Recuperating, he decides to go to a coffeehouse where he can sit and read the paper. There his eyes are drawn to the window next to him that gives on to the street, where he idly watches the usual varied crowd of people passing; gamblers, peddlers, beggars, invalids, prostitutes, and day laborers. Suddenly his attention is riveted on an old man. His clothes, though filthy, are of good quality; he looks intelligent. Specific characteristics are engraved on his face: greed, malice, gaiety, terror, despair, caution, and bloodthirstiness. He is carrying a diamond

and a dagger. Although it is raining, the narrator feels
so drawn to him that he leaves the café and follows
the aged fellow for the next two days through all
types of neighborhoods. (We must be here as elsewhere aware of the fact that fantasy dominates.)
Never once, however, does he see his pursuer, not
even when the narrator accosts him and looks him
straight in the eye. Exhausted finally, the narrator
gives up his search, reasoning: "This old man is the
type and the genius of deep crime." The narrator
can learn nothing from him that he does not already
know.

At the outset of his search, the narrator is intent
on discovering something about the old man, that
mysterious shadowy being who emerges from the
street as night is deepening. Prior to this event he
had been ill and housebound; he had to go to the
café, to the street, the outer world to find an answer
to his problem.

The café, a kind of bridge between the inner
and outer worlds, gives him what he cannot grasp
either in his books or his newspaper, an element
that must be lived to be understood. It is at night
that he first sees the old man, when the gas lamps
are lit, when the "wild effects of light" come into
being and play on facial features. Then a face
emerges from blackness, as does a dream or a
thought that bursts into consciousness. The narrator
is not only struck by the old man he sees outside
the café, but he is fascinated and even mesmerized.
"How wild a story, I said to myself, is written within
that bosom!" Why should he be so taken by this old
man? What is the reason for his fascination?

Just as every quality has its opposite, so every
person casts a shadow if there is sufficient light.
Since the advent of Christianity, the shadow and
darkness generally have been equated with evil and

instinctual animal nature, considered to be disorganized and chaotic, something to be ruled and controlled if not entirely overcome. The Christian's denial of this shadow force—the "animal" within—serves only to repress this power, to keep it submerged.

The qualities seen in the old man's countenance, which include acumen, cautiousness, penuriousness, greed, maliciousness, and despair among others (not all considered evil) take on the attributes for the narrator of a primordial image. The aged figure becomes so highly charged an autonomous center of power that he dominates the narrator's conscious personality and sweeps him out into the street, indicating that he is engulfed by some inner vision. During the night hours, when consciousness recedes and dreams take over, the narrator becomes a prey to his own inner imagery. As in a dream, he has no idea where he is going. He loses his way in unfamiliar neighborhoods. Everything becomes different, confused, and new as symbolically he penetrates more deeply into the corridors of his own mind.

A younger man's identification with a much older one most frequently is associated with a desire for authority, law, and order, a return to a regularized state, to which the narrator evidently tries to relate. Perhaps Poe may be thinking about his own relationship with Allan and his change of heart insofar as he was concerned. A whole world of imponderables comes into being. Why, for example, does the aged figure rush about so frantically, and why does the narrator continue to follow him? In both cases, extreme intensity is evident—a need to investigate and explore. But as is characteristic of an archetypal image, the old man extends beyond the image of a personal father and stems from the collective domain. That the narrator is recuperating from an illness indicates a depletion of energy on his part, a need to acquire vital strength again. In some strange way, the aged gentleman, he senses, will fulfill this need. The confrontation between the two indicates a facing of the aging process which the narrator previously has been unable to do. He has been seriously ill. The spiritual isolation, the wasting of his body, and the feared outcome have isolated him. Seated in the café, imprisoned in his mental outlook, set behind the window that separates him from the street and the crowd, he sees that old strange figure and rushes out hoping that his dead and dying soul will be renewed by the very human vitality of this old fellow.

When, however, the narrator finally faces the old man and there is no sign of recognition, he ceases his pursuit and remains "absorbed in contemplation." No longer tyrannized by some dormant element within himself, he realizes that what he glimpsed in the night is too powerful a factor for him to cope with. Something within him has stirred and compelled him to stop his search. The old man "is the type of genius of deep crime," he now understands, and to get too close to him might bring about his own death. This sort of man, he reasons, "refuses to be alone. *He is the man of the crowd.*" There is no pat conclusion to be drawn from "The Man of the Crowd" except that in attempting to understand the shadow—a face in the crowd in this instance—one may be confronted with facelessness, with the one lost in the many. Under such conditions, it may be better to question no further unless one is strong enough to explore one's depths, that collective unconscious where individuality no longer exists and where one may experience a cleansing and a *renewal* but where one also risks the terrible danger of losing one's ego in the process. The mystery in "The Man of the Crowd" remains, despite the fact that the shadow figure of the old man simply sinks back into the unconscious to remain hidden and unexplored until revitalized and reborn in another eerie surreal tale.

"The Masque of the Red Death" (1842)

Plague is used here as a catalyst. Poe may have been inspired to write this tale as an aftermath to the cholera epidemic that raged in Baltimore in the summer of 1831. The collective evil or shadow projection is symbolized by the "red" plague that divests people of their blood and diminishes their vital essence, yielding them up to the onslaught of illness and death.

To counteract this dread situation after the outbreak of the plague, Prince Prospero gathers a thousand knights and ladies of his court into one of his abbeys. He makes certain that his new dwelling place is well stocked in every respect, and he believes it to be entirely impregnable to any evil of body or soul. After some months, to further the mood of conviviality, he decides to give a masked ball. Clowns, dancers, and musicians are hired to heighten the festivities that are to take place in seven different adjoining rooms, each lit by a different color: blue, purple, green, white, violet, and red, with the last room being furnished entirely in black. A huge ebony clock tolls the hours.

At midnight a strange figure appears, shrouded like a corpse and wearing a mask covered with blood. Prospero, angered at the sight, pursues alone this phantomlike figure, for all his guests are terrified and do not follow at first. Presently they realize, however, that a struggle is taking place; and when they arrive at the spot in question, they find the prince dead. When they attempt to seize the intruder-murderer, who stands "erect and motionless within the shadow of the ebony clock," they gasp "in unutterable horror at finding the grave-cerements and corpse-like mask which they handle with so violent a rudeness, untenanted by any tangible form." Realizing then that the plague has indeed penetrated their domain, they die one by one: "And Darkness and Decay and the Red Death held illimitable dominion over all."

Regarded symbolically, epidemics, plagues, and contagious illnesses are manifestations of psychic illness and social imbalance, of functions that have gone awry or temporarily broken down in the collective sphere. An ancient example of this is the plight of Thebes that occurred after Oedipus assumed the throne. Factors incompatible with conscious attitudes then take precedence and become visible in the form of physical illness and psychogenic symptoms of every kind. To seek to stifle or bury such psychic forces or to try to wall them off in dungeon or prison cells or even in a palace serves only to increase anxiety and tension, to build up their explosive quality.

The illnesses that occur in many of Poe's tales represent the unhealthy nature of the ruling principle that exists within his protagonists' psyches. Epidemics are highly contagious and spread like wildfire, like blood coursing through the body or like evil in the world. Similarly, when shadow characteristics exist potently in an individual, the demonic effects radiate outward. The energy implicit in a negative outlook demolishes the rational function and triggers a lowering of the rational attitude within both individuals and groups. People huddle together in times of crisis, uniting to ward off the common enemy, whereas in peaceable circumstances, they often sneer at and despise each other. There seems to be a binding anagogic power that comes into being during threatening precarious times.

That Prospero, this young ruler, chooses to withdraw along with his knights and ladies into an abbey to avoid a confrontation with his feared enemy, the Red Death, indicates a desire and a will to act, but to act in the inner and not the outer sphere. The abbey, representing a religious and cloistered view, represents an unnatural way of life. For Prospero it is used to dispel the all-powerful Masque of Death. Though he seeks "religion's" protection by withdrawing into its confines, he does not adhere to its rules and disciplines and instead lives out his merrymaking routine in the cloister. Thus, he can be assured of no help with regard to acquisition of a new and healthful spiritual attitude.

The seven rooms, each differently colored, set the tone for the scenes: blue represents celestial ways; purple, regal attitudes; and black, of course, death. The number seven may be looked upon as a cosmic center: the seven planetary spheres, the seven notes of the scale, each functioning as a unit yet related to the others as a whole. The rooms represent the evolution of the plague's destructive powers: the reverse of the seven days of Creation. Like Dante's trajectory in Inferno, so the dancers will revel their lives away from dream to reality, life to death.

Blood, as implied in the title of Poe's tale and as a reality at its conclusion, is often associated with the Christian Last Supper, the Crucifixion, and the holy grail, or the chalice in which Joseph of Arimathea preserved Christ's blood. Blood is symbolic of life itself, both physical and spiritual; it is certainly true that at the conclusion of Poe's tale, blood implies only death. The protagonist's "vesture was dabbled in blood—and his broad brow, with all the features of the face, was besprinkled with the scarlet horror."

There is no question but that the figure standing "motionless within the shadow of the ebony clock" is death and thus is identified with the instrument that marks the hours. Time has been personified in innumerable legends and literary works with an old man: Father Time, decrepit, aged, waiting with his scythe to grasp his victims.

That time plays such a major part in this tale illustrates the impossibility of staying terrestrial, temporal change. Even during the course of Christ's crucifixion, for example, the three long hours were marked out by the crowing of the cock; here too, the "pendulum" swings to and fro, and the revelers, listening to the "dull, heavy, monotonous clang" emanating from its "brazen lungs," fear the "sound which was clear and loud and deep and exceedingly musical." So strange and terrifying is the clock's strike that even the musicians stop their music and the waltzers cease their dance each time its clanging tonality shatters the atmosphere. It is through the passing of time, as struck by the clock, that one sometimes comes to understand the significance of timeless life and may awaken to the realization of an afterlife. The sounding of the pendulum with its own special knell acts as a link between the two worlds: visible and invisible, known and unknown, consciousness and unconsciousness, life and death.

Only when the clock marks the death knell, the hour of midnight, does the dancing cease. Then the inescapable and immutable archetype of the Red Death joins the group, causing fear and trembling; it symbolizes the very real need for integrating the temporal forces that it personifies. Prospero alone faces the mask of death in a style and way that the protagonist in "The Man of the Crowd" was unable to do, and is killed.

Death, as concretized in this tale, represents the end of a stage in life. To face such extinction is to come to terms with the very fact of change and decay, of birth and growth, light and darkness. In "The Masque of the Red Death," however, death does not imply a rebirth. Resurrection and transmutation are not in the offing here, and neither are liberation and evolution. Death is simply a killer, a negating form that stands for decomposition, for the cessation of life with no hope of a world beyond. The tale ends in the seventh room, the room of blackness and blood, reminiscent of pain and suffering and not of the greenness that garbs the earth in the spring with its bounty and fruitfulness.

"The Pit and the Pendulum" (1843)

Poe's most harrowing tale of terror, "The Pit and the Pendulum," which has a surprise ending, describes a descent into the depths of the unconscious, a confrontation with the shadow personality.

The narrator in this tale is a victim of the Spanish Inquisition. The religious persecution—investigation and punishment for so-called heresy—known as the Inquisition took place in Spain, Portugal, Germany, and the Papal States. Started in 1233, it did not actually end until early in the nineteenth century. Its most dreadful and intensive period occurred between the thirteenth and sixteenth centuries, when the hierarchy of the Roman Catholic Church condemned heretics to imprisonment and death. The Spanish Inquisition, which began in 1478, was particularly cruel in that in many cases even those only accused of heresy were tortured and burned at the stake. This tale of Poe's, therefore, does not deal with natural evil but with evil perpetrated by supposedly civilized and self-avowedly devout members of the human race.

The narrator of "The Pit and the Pendulum" is a survivor of the Spanish Inquisition who was sentenced to torture and death. He is imprisoned in a dungeon cell beneath the surface of the earth. Shortly after being placed there, he loses consciousness. When he regains his lucidity sometime later, he looks at the darkness around him and is overwhelmed by terror. Slowly, his natural emotional reaction begins to ebb, and he starts to analyze his situation and to examine the surrounding torture chamber. Although shadows intervene, he is able to make out a deep and seemingly bottomless pit into which he has almost fallen as he moves about. Overcome with fatigue, he finally falls asleep and awakens to find that some bread and water have been placed beside him. He eats and drinks and then lapses back into a comatose state. He regains consciousness and realizes that he has been drugged and that his body is now bound to a wooden frame, with rats slithering around him. He gazes at the ceiling and sees a pendulum swinging above him, a foot-long crescent knifelike instrument slowly descending with a measured downward movement. Time passes. Then, while the blade of the pendulum is about to pierce his chest, he realizes that if he is to survive he must proceed logically and use all the resources of his conscious mind. He begins smearing the ropes that bind him with the food. The rats swarm over him as they eat the food, and in so doing they gnaw through the ropes that hold him fast. Freed, he slides from beneath the descending blade of the pendulum only to realize that the iron walls of his cell are growing steadily hotter and moving in on him; he is being forced closer and closer to the edge of the pit.

The darkness, which may be said to be a hallmark of Poe's tales of terror, represents in this instance a positive value. For the alchemist, a condition of blackness implies chaos: comparable to the Gnostic's "Primal Darkness," an undifferentiated and unknowable realm. The narrator is imprisoned in his archaic world which may be thought of as the collective unconscious. From this vantage point he must attempt to cope with his problems. In these black depths the narrator learns to function and to prevent disintegration and death. Fear exists mainly because there is the brink of an open pit into which he is so close to plunging and a suffocating sense of dread as he sees no way of escape from his incarceration. Now he uses his reasoning powers to find a way to escape. In "The Black Cat," the narrator is unable to follow the path of conscious reason; he reacts instinctively, striking out at whatever he feels hostility for. In "The Pit and the Pendulum," the narrator's return to the Womb or the Mother Earth, paves the way for a rebirth.

The original predicament of the narrator symbolizes that of the inner being which at first is unable to see any lighter areas in the primal blackness. As he explores his situation as rationally as he can, he is in effect encountering his shadow and attempts to deal with it. It is at this crucial point that his conscious mind comes to the rescue and saves him from being overwhelmed.

He is given bread by his torturers which he believes to be drugged. The potion inserted in the food or water is not noxious; it merely makes him sleep. The profound sleep which he is now experiencing enables him to come into contact with the deepest

levels of his psyche, endowing him with the strength
to deal with the awesome dangers that threaten his
life.

Upon awakening, the narrator's fear of losing
his life is viewed more logically; he divides his
problems into segments, analyzes his plight, and
determines the best way out of it. Sometimes, however, when one believes to have overcome all obstacles, the most frightening experience may come
to pass, as in Poe's tale. The iron walls grow fiery
hot and move closer to the protagonist, forcing him
nearer to the drop in the pit, the abyss from which
there is no hope of return. The narrator grasps at the
horror of his situation. What he does not know is
that he is being observed from above. Just as life is
about to be swept away from him, a *deus ex machina*
ending occurs. He hears voices, among them that of
General Lasalle, whose French armies have stayed
the forces of the Inquisition. The narrator is rescued.

"The Tell-Tale Heart" (1843)

Although at the outset of "The Tell-Tale Heart" Poe
takes great pains to tell the reader that he is not
dealing with a mental case, the unfolding drama is
nevertheless concerned with a pathological condition. Poe was always fascinated with alienation and
mental disease and familiar with the great strides
made in the treatment of the insane in the second
half of the eighteenth century. Before then large
hospitals let their patients vegetate in dungeonlike
cellar areas or lunatic towers. Those who were incarcerated there were awash with filth when they
were not being bled, purged, or immersed in ice-
cold water in an attempt to shock them into their
senses. Thanks to the groundbreaking work of Phi-

lippe Pinel, who no longer tied his patients down or enchained them, a kinder therapy was instituted at La Salpêtrière hospital, and there patients had a good chance of recovery.[23] Poe must have been familiar with their innovations.

The narrator of "The Tell-Tale Heart" may well be criminally insane. From the very outset, he complains of a sharpening of his senses, particularly the sense of hearing. He wonders whether such an alteration in perception can explain the events that have taken place. He confesses that he loved the old man whom he slew; it was only something about the gaze of the old man that inexplicably disturbed him. He had "the eye of a vulture—a pale blue eye, with a film over it," and each time it gazed at the narrator, the latter's blood ran cold. He could no longer stand the sight of this all-piercing force. For seven nights the narrator crept into the old man's room while he slept, intent on killing him. But since the man's eyes were closed, he felt unable to do the deed.

In this tale, the eye is viewed as an observing consciousness, seeking to illuminate, to judge what the narrator seeks to keep dark and hidden. To face the eye is to view one's entire life span. To see with this organ of perception and truth is to be confronted with what one really is. That the narrator is virtually paralyzed when considering this power indicates his unwillingness to look into his own terrifying shadow world.

That these eyes are those of an old man whom he believes he loves but in reality hates is also significant. As a father archetype, the narrator sees him as a kind of Kronos figure, a father who devours his own children so that he will never be replaced by them. The narrator's attitude toward him is ambivalent, and understandably so. The old man is a lovable person, but he is also in a position to destroy him. What he represents is to the narrator both retrogressive and intolerable.

Comparable to a vulture, the narrator feels, this pale-blue force is following him everywhere, lying in wait for him. It may unmask him and force him to face the fact that he is a failure in life, and he finds his fury growing to maniacal proportions.

It is at night, when the unconscious reigns and the hallucinatory world is all fear and terror, when ghosts and ghouls outline themselves in a pitch-black room, when consciousness recedes and fears dictate one's acts, that the narrator visits the old man's room. For seven nights he goes there and the old man is always asleep. Then, on the eighth, he opens the door and finds him sitting up in bed, frightened, "the groan of mortal terror" emanating from him. The narrator opens the door a little more, only enough to permit a glimmer of light to intrude; "like the thread of the spider, shot from out the crevice," it falls upon "the vulture eye." At this moment, "It was open-wide, wide open—and I grew furious as I gazed upon it." What increases the narrator's anger further is the "dull, quick sound, such as a watch makes when enveloped in cotton" emanating from the old man's rapidly beating heart. Unlike Perseus, who drugged the Medusa and then cut off her head, the narrator in Poe's tale commits his crime when the eye is wide open and staring at him. After the deed he dismembers the corpse and buries it neatly under three floor planks in the old man's bedroom. "I then replaced the boards so cleverly, so cunningly, that no human eye—not even *his*—could have detected anything wrong."

Poe's maniacal narrator is possessed by a phobia. His murder of the aged figure—a dismemberment ritual—is really self-destructive. He is cutting out what he cannot stand in the old man, that vulture eye which brings him turmoil and suffering. By burying the parts of the dead man under the floor boards, he believes erroneously that he will escape retribution.

When three policemen enter the home, having been called to investigate a scream heard in the vicinity, the narrator tells them that he frequently cries out in his sleep. He shows them the old man's room, now neat and tidy, and tells them the old man has gone to the country. For some unknown reason, however, they stay on, and it is at this point that the narrator begins hearing a ringing in his ears, a pounding as though a watch were beating ever more loudly. Unable to stand this noise, he confesses to his crime. The wooden planks are removed, the parts of the body found, and the narrator apprehended.

Few of Poe's narrators understood the meaning of the heart: the sphere of feeling. They have so repressed it as to have virtually excised it from their being. Tantalized by this force that apparently paves the way for the love-hate principle, the narrator in "The Tell-Tale Heart" hears only its physical pounding and cannot integrate what it represents. He therefore resents it, and it becomes that "other," that enemy, that shadow force which he feels he must eradicate but that will haunt him always. It is only when he is incarcerated in the solitude of the prison or mental institution to which he is assigned that he begins to explore and weigh the cause of the murder he committed.

"The Imp of the Perverse" (1845)

"The Imp of the Perverse" takes the reader into the domain of evil. "We tremble with the violence of

the conflict within us—of the definite with the in-
definite—of the substance with the shadow," declares the narrator of the tale. Why, then, he questions, do some people feel the necessity to stand at
the edge of a precipice and "peer into the abyss" or
even throw themselves down into it? Why do they
seek punishment, torture, agony? For months the
narrator of "The Imp of the Perverse" planned the
perfect murder, and then he committed it. No one
suspected him of anything, and he could have lived
on peacefully to the end of his days had he not felt
himself suffocating: "I became blind, and deaf, and
giddy; and then, some invisible fiend, I thought
struck me with his broad palm upon the back. The
long imprisoned secret burst forth from my soul,"
and the dreadful deed was apprehended.

That perversity plays a vast part in the narrator's
personality must be conceded, but efforts to discover
what causes such ill functioning in the brain are still
fruitless. Poe mentions in the tale the attempts of
phrenologists to discover the complexities of the inner man. The system of Franz Joseph Gall was the
subject of a lecture given in Richmond, Virginia, in
1824 by George A. Stevens. Gall believed that regions of the brain could be correlated with certain
of its functions; each convolution, for example, had
its own capacity and significance. The topography
of the brain could therefore provide information on
a person's propensities and character traits. Each
protruberance in the skull and each bulge around
the ear suggest specific characteristics which Gall
described. Poe's narrator, however, remains uncon-
vinced of the efficacy of this method. The system
seems too pat.

Moralists are also held in contempt by Poe's
narrator; those who believe that life is a struggle between good and evil and that one must constantly

be vigilant to root out or force down the negative or shadow characteristics in the world. Psychologists would say that the shadow, if properly understood and accepted, can be integrated into the personality and in this manner transformed into a healthy positive force.

Nor is the Cartesian point of view well thought of in Poe's tale. The seventeenth-century French philosopher believed that the rational faculty was God-given and that the exercise of it was the only valid answer to the insurmountable questions that confront human beings. By perfecting reason, Descartes suggested, man would expand his knowledge and eventually solve the riddles of nature and conquer it. Poe's narrator, however, rejects the "arrogance of reason" which is symptomatic of Descartes's thinking.

The rational and irrational worlds are at odds in "The Imp of the Perverse." A double personality emerges as the narrator probes the meaning of his actions. He has lived as a respectable member of the middle class for years. Yet some foreign element, a feeling, a thought, seems to have crept up on him; the imp, an offspring of the devil perhaps, has apparently grafted itself upon his inner being. This imp has fed on unknown sources within him, has gained in strength, and now has forced its needs upon the narrator. It refuses to stay dormant within the unconscious but progressively encroaches on territories outside. The ego as a result can no longer mediate between the inner and outer worlds, nor can it function as a mediator between rational and irrational spheres. A split has occurred, a dissociation of the personality.

The narrator's compulsion to confess his crime indicates that his pride in his cunning and reasoning power has inflated, and experiences its success in the vainest of ways. Indeed, the narrator feels a kind of "giddiness" within him, as though he has succeeded in the most incredible of feats and longs to boast of his deed to the world. To tell of his great prowess indicates a deep-seated sense of inferiority, a morbid pride.

For some people, particularly of the Judeo-Christian tradition, expiation and suffering have been ritualized and play a great role in the process of repentance and atonement. Those believers who practice disciplines grow aware of the impact of their acts and thoughts on themselves and others—or so they believe. Some seek martyrdom, hoping to eradicate their solipsistic ways by abnegating the ego but also by trying to emulate Christ, thereby gaining salvation. Poe's narrator, although he feels the necessity of revealing his crime, knowing he will be punished for it, does so gratuitously. He is not seeking to purge himself of evil. It is not the killing that disturbed him; on the contrary, he sought the world's approbation and admiration for his brilliant accomplishment. What he failed to realize was the consequence of this knowledge. When a demonic force enters the psyche, it acts according to its own logic; it emerges freely of its own volition, without consulting the rational function, and sometimes appears at the most inopportune moment. It is this uncontrollable undeveloped factor within the narrator—his adolescent side, that forces the revelation of the crime and so inflicts punishment on him.

Rather than leading to better adaptation to the subjective inner and hence to the objective outer world—the narrator remains unfeeling concerning his crime and the punishment he undergoes. He unearths no new values.

'The Cask of Amontillado" (1846)

"The Cask of Amontillado" is a study in revenge
and murder which shows to what lengths the rational
function will go in perpetrating the most evil deeds.
The tale takes place during the carnival period in
Italy, perhaps near Rome. During these festive hours
inhibitions are relaxed and instincts unleashed.
Montresor, the protagonist, bears a grudge against
Fortunato, for having insulted him some time in the
past. When Montresor meets Fortunato during the
carnival, he plans his revenge. Knowing him to be
a connoisseur of spirits, he tells Fortunato that he
has some very rare Amontillado wine. He invites
him to his family palace to taste this Amontillado.
Fortunato agrees; he follows his "friend" down to
the wine cellar. The dripping dampness and increasingly colder temperature are no longer felt by
him because of the samplings of different wines
which the host offers his guest as they proceed down
the circular staircase. By the time the two reach the
bottom of the vault, Fortunato is so inebriated that
he is unaware of his surroundings and of the fact
that Montresor has chained him up in a niche and
then immured him with the trowel and fresh mortar
he had placed there. When Fortunato finally sobers
up and realizes what has happened, he begs to be
released. But no one hears him. His bones have remained there undisturbed, the narrator informs the
reader, for the past fifty years.

Poe's propensity for the descent into moist,
mossy, and fungal recesses is never better displayed
than in "The Cask of Amontillado": "We passed
through a range of low arches, descended, passed
on, and descending again, arrived at a crypt in which
the foulness of the air caused our flambeaux rather
to glow than to flame." Descents sometimes imply

a need to regress to primeval levels, to archaic substrata, to vegetative spheres where life is experienced in its most basic way and differentiation has
not yet come into being. Cain too went underground
after the murer of his brother Abel and, according
to the Kabbalah, founded the city of Enochia and
invented the art of metallurgy. Unlike Cain, Montresor descends the winding inner staircase not to
suffer martyrdom but to inflict it upon another, to
punish and destroy that person who has ridiculed
and injured him.

The narrator's need to enchain and immure his
enemy, to wall him up in these vaulted areas and
separate him from the outside world, reveals the
power of the forces at stake, those emotions compelling him to enact his murderous deed. Montresor
cannot deal with his rage and awaits the carnival
season, when a spirit of liberation dulls the rational
function, to commit his crime.

That wine, Amontillado in particular, which is
a variety of fine dry sherry from Spain, should have
been the vehicle used to dull consciousness symbolizes the impotence of cerebrality. No longer "ar-
rogant," as it once was in "The Imp of the Perverse,"
it was contained and accepted. Wine is the domain
of Dionysus: blood, youth, those moments of divine
intoxication when joy expands consciousness and
overtakes the tragedy with which some associate the
empirical world. Wine is the food of ecstasy and
leads to orgiastic pleasures; it is also a sacramental
offering. Blood and wine have been linked throughout history; each in its own way allows for visions
of heightened reality, for an epiphany. He who
drinks of it is allowed unlimited energy, spiritual
and physical. Under its influence, conscience and
consciousness vanish, guilt is assuaged, and revenge,
anger, and passions of all kinds are nullified.

Fortunato has been reduced to the vegetative world, the primeval level of intellectual rot and decay. It is here that the exploration ceases; as Montresor says at the conclusion of the tale, let his revenge *"In pace resquiescat!"*

In each of Poe's shadow tales we are taken on a Dantesque journey into an inferno, made privy to the tortuous world of personalities who have not been able to integrate their shadows, who feel the need to punish or be punished, to earn redemption or be oblivious to such feelings. In most cases, a desire to flaunt a morbid pride is obvious. Most of Poe's shadow figures are like automata, instruments of the mind, guided by some superintellectual force [or being]; they feel nothing, no warmth or compassion for another human being. Poe's creatures are projections of unconscious drives and are not flesh and blood.

Nor do they offer values. No judgmental forces are at work. Crime is neither a negative nor a positive act. Poe's psychopaths do not distinguish between good and evil, nor do they usually feel remorse or guilt. They are dominated by the shadow archetype, a primeval force which compels them to transgress. Their success often causes them to experience delusions of grandeur and so powerful an enthusiasm as to blind them to see the dangers involved when they flaunt their prowess, thus demanding society's retribution.

The extremes of mood of many of Poe's narrators bring to mind a condition that Heraclitus called *enantiodromia*: the law of opposites that causes the psyche to veer from one extreme to another, from lethargy to hyperactivity, joy to sorrow, reason to instinct, love to hate. What is of importance here is the tension in the psyche's regulatory system. When, for example, the narrator in "The Imp of the Perverse" identifies with reason alone, the instinctual world is aroused and demands attention; because it has been deprived of its right, it resorts to any lengths to acquire it.

To try to eliminate the instinctual sphere from the psyche only nourishes its power; the attempt to obliterate the shadow leads often in Poe's tales to monomania and obsessions of many kinds, even to murder. When such a murderous escapade is terminated depression frequently sets in with the realization that the crime has not led to the expected relief. The dazed and crazed emotions that followed the act have been whipped up to such a frenzy that they are confused with a kind of joy, with hubris. A fall followed these heights; the mask was sheared; the moment when the narrator has to face the emptiness of his ways, the identitylessness of his psyche, and the elongated shadow it casts came to pass— and the tale was born as a result.

The Mystical Quest

Throughout his life, Poe found it difficult to adapt to the outside world. He could not face the ugliness of the burgeoning industrial civilization rising about him. As an orphan, with no social standing and without financial means, he was unable to relate to people or to a mercantile society.[24] Alone and solitary, he withdrew into his own subjective world, a realm. pulsating with anima and shadow figures ranging from the defenseless to the strong, the cruel to the kind. There existed also another world for Poe in which he immersed himself as a relief from his own churning thoughts and feelings, a Utopian sphere where he experienced transcendence and the godhead's immanence.

Poe was highly skeptical of any organized answers to metaphysical problems. He did not share
Emerson's "obscure" brand of transcendentalism or
Emerson's views concerning a "Supreme Mind or
Over-Soul." In his essay "Ralph Waldo Emerson,"
Poe wrote: "Mr. Ralph Waldo Emerson belongs to
a class of gentlemen with whom we have no patience
whatever—the mystics for mysticism's sake." Poe
was far more attuned to the outlook of such contemporaries as Hawthorne, Emily Dickinson, and Her-
man Melville, who held no brief for organized religion and who cut their ties at least covertly with
conventional Protestant belief but who explored religious themes in their writings and were as fascinated as he by questions of the relationship between
body and mind and between appearance and reality.
"It is by no means an irrational fancy," Poe wrote
in *Marginalia*, that in a future existence "we shall
look upon what we think our present existence, as
a dream."

Poe was greatly influenced by Swedenborg,
who claimed to have communciated with the souls
of the departed, with saints and angels and also believed in clairvoyance. He displayed his powers in
London in 1759, when he described the burning of
Stockholm at the very moment it was taking place.

Poe was also much impressed by the theories
of Anton Mesmer and read all he could about his
experiments and those of his disciple Jacques de
Puységur. Many psychological discoveries were indeed made. Puységur, for example, became aware
of the fact that forgotten memories of the past that
could not be recollected when awake could be
evoked during a hypnotic trance. This condition,
known as hyperamnesia, paved the way for what has
been referred to as privileged moments of extralucid
manifestations. The universal fluid pervading the

cosmos made it possible, it was believed, to perceive
faraway events, even those taking place on different
continents, and to predict the future as well. Such
increased lucidity and the somnambulist's ability to
experience various planes of consciousness enables
communication between the individual and the *all*
or world soul.[25]

Also explored were dreams, visions, delusions,
idées fixe, phobias, and sleep walking. E. T. A.
Hoffmann's "The Devil's Elixir" might also be used
as a scientific guide explaining the virtues of hypnotism. Balzac's *Louis Lambert, Ursule Mirouët*, and
Seraphita Seraphitus deal with extrasensory perception, schizophrenia, and clairvoyance. Novalis's
Hymns to the Night and his *Disciples of Saïs* probe
the realm of death and the world of ancient mysteries. Nerval's "Sylvie" and "Angélique" resound
with the occult and the realm of metempsychosis—
the transmigration of the soul after death to some
other body.

Poe felt a deep-seated affinity with eighteenth-
and nineteenth-century occultists and mystics. He
was drawn to the extraordinary, to the atemporal
realm in which he believed and which bore him out
of the inferno of his own splintered existence. In a
number of his tales, he called forth a whole world
of evanescent spirits, a lighter realm with its haunting and tender notes. In "The Island of the Fay"
(1841) and "The Domain of Arnheim" (1847), death
did not mean annihilation, but was coupled with a
belief in reincarnation, with eternal life, and thus a
sort of paradise. His attitude toward nature was most
moving; it revealed his need to communicate with
the world soul, with divinity; then he could give his
feelings free reign, a condition denied him in daily
life. "I love, indeed, to regard the dark valleys, and
the grey rocks, and the waters that silently smile,

and the forests that sigh in uneasy slumbers, and the proud watchful mountains that look down upon all— I love to regard these as themselves but the colossal members of one vast animate and sentient whole," he wrote in "The Island of the Fay."

Poe's mysticism, unlike that of Dom Pernetty or Claude de St. Martin or Swedenborg, does not teach submission to the will of God, nor does it suggest certain disciplines and rituals around which the above-mentioned mystics built their religious systems. Poe seeks union with God in a pantheistic embrace, in nature itself, which he looked upon as divine. He grasps ultimate reality in the forces before him: a mountain, grass, tree, flower. These entities feed his feelings and nurture his passions. As he looks about—at the mountains and stars, the earth and branches of trees, the tarns and bogs—he discovers endless and seemingly infinite space.

As we find cycle within cycle without end—yet all revolving around one far-distant centre which is the godhead, may we not analogically suppose, in the same manner, life within life, the less within the greater, and all within the Spirit Divine? In short, we are madly erring, through self-esteem, in believing man, in either his temporal or future destinies, to be of more moment in the universe than that vast "clod of the valley" which he tills and contemns, and to which he denies a soul for no more profound reason than that he does not behold it in operation (p. 281).

Nature underscores for Poe the notion of cosmic correspondences as enunciated by Hermes Trismegistus and Swedenborg, along with such mystics as Jakob Boehme and Meister Eckhart. In "The Island of the Fay" we read:

The shade of the trees fell heavily upon the water, and seemed to bury itself therein, impregnating the depths of the element with darkness. I fancied that each shadow, as the sun descended lower and lower, separated itself sullenly from the trunk that gave it birth, and thus absorbed by the stream; while other shadows issued momentarily from the trees, taking the place of their predecessors thus entombed (p. 282).

Nature offered Poe sustenance for his psyche as well as for his aesthetic sense with its ordered designs, its admixtures of fluidity and concretion, and its tonalities and silences. In "The Domain of Arnheim" he verbally orchestrated his feelings:

There is a gush of entrancing melody; there is an oppressive sense of strange-sweet odor;—there is a dreamlike intermingling to the eye of tall slender Eastern trees—bosky shrubberies—flocks of golden and crimson birds—lily-fringed lakes—meadows of violets, tulips, poppies, hyacinths and tuberoses—long intertangled lines of silver streamlets—and, upspringing confusedly from amid all, a semi-Gothic, semi-Saracenic architecture, sustaining itself as if by a miracle in mid-air, glittering in the red sunlight with a hundred oriels, minarets, and pinnacles; and seeming the phantom handiwork, cojointly, of the Sylphs, of the Fairies, *of the Genii*, and of the Gnomes (p. 556).

Poe's aesthetic sensibilities made for a *unio mystica* with nature, with the *all*. Such an affinity is in sharp contrast with the cruel actions and crushing hatreds seen in his shadow figures and the depersonalization in this anima images. In nature Poe seems to have found an inner light that bathed and purified him, a force that allowed him to feel an affinity with cosmic vibrations, making him part of life's rhythm. No longer isolated, he could participate in nature's grand design and not be alienated from it. It is in this sense that Poe was religious, that is, in the original Latin meaning of the word *religio*, a binding or relinking into the very heart of being where one experiences the universal soul, the cosmic oneness.

"Metzengerstein" (1836)

"Metzengerstein," the first of Poe's stories to be published, broaches the question of metempsychosis and synchronicity, both phenomena that occur in a world far beyond the Newtonian empirical one of cause and effect, a realm which takes the reader into the unknown.

The tale itself may have stemmed from a dream or been the manifestation of a trauma. The setting is feudal Hungary, the land of gypsies and vampires. It relates the story of the last descendants of two illustrious nobel families—the Berlifitzings and the Metzengersteins—who have been feuding with each other for centuries. An old doddering count is the sole survivor of one family; a debauched and cruel young baron, of the other. One night, for some unknown reason, Count Berlifitzing's stables have caught fire and are burning out of control along with the count's prize horses. During these events, Baron Metzengerstein happens to be seated in meditation in an upper apartment in his castle. He is staring at a tapestry in front of him on which is portrayed one of his ancestors mounted on a fiery steed and slaying a Berlifitzing. As the baron gazes at the rider and horse, the horse's eyes suddenly seem to move and stare directly at him. The baron is terrified and runs toward the door.

As he threw it open, a flash of red light, streaming far into the chamber, flung his shadow with a clear outline against the quivering tapestry; and he shuddered to perceive that shadow—as he staggered a while upon the threshold—assuming the exact position, and precisely filling up the contour, of the relentless and triumphant murderer of the Saracen Berlifitzing (p. 95).

The baron rushes outdoors, hoping that the fresh air will clear his head. At this very instant, a groom enters the castle grounds, holding a gigantic steed, the duplicate of the one portrayed in the tapestry. It has escaped from the Berlifitzing stables, the groom informs him. Meanwhile, another servant tells of a strange happening within the castle: part of the tapestry featuring a steed and its rider, the one the baron had seen when meditating, has been cut out. The death of the old Count Berlifitzing is now announced; seemingly he had tried to rescue some of his horses from his burning stables, and the effort had killed him. Thereafter Baron Metzengerstein spends his time riding on the mysterious and nameless steed which had been brought to him under such strange circumstances. One stormy night sometime later, when he has galloped off with maniacal speed, he returns to see his own castle aflame. He rides into the gateway, mounts the staircase to the very top, and is never seen again. "A white flame still enveloped the building like a shroud, and streaming far away into the quiet atmosphere, shot forth a glare or preternatural light; while a cloud of smoke settled heavily over the battlements in the distinct colossal figure of—a *horse*."

Psychokinesis, the power of the mind to move a physical object without the aid of mechanical means, and synchronicity, which lie at the heart of "Metzengerstein," were popular literary subjects throughout the eighteenth and nineteenth centuries: Jacques Cazotte's *Devil in Love*, Théophile Gautier's *Fantastic Tales*, E. T. A. Hoffmann's *Night Pieces* and *Fantasy Pieces*, Balzac's "The Red Inn, and Nerval's "The Enchanted Hand" are only some of the many works that explore these themes. The question of metempsychosis, which has always fascinated those unable to accept that death brings an end to human life, is one way of dealing with the subject of immortality.

The first strange happening occurred when the
baron, meditating in his room and perhaps experiencing a kind of self-hypnosis, has an optical illusion
and sees the horse in the tapestry coming to life and
looking directly at him. The steed is associated with
one of his glorious ancestors with whom he identifies: the pride and power depicted in both man
and beast put him in touch with his own inner world,
activating a kind of rapport between himself and the
domain of things, objects lower than the human
sphere, nevertheless, animate according to mystics.

Why should a horse have been the vehicle for
this psychokinetic experience and for the synchronistic happening to follow? The horse represents instinct, libido, and power. The image of riding upon
this animal indicates an ability to control and command. The Wagnerian god Wotan galloped amid
turbulent storms, and Siegfried is said to have leaped
over a wall of fire on his thunder horse Grani. Horses
are also endowed with other attributes: clairvoyance
and the ability to peer into mysterious worlds.

In Poe's tale, both forces are at work: the con-
quering horse and the one that can see into the future. The horse possesses what the baron himself
would like to have: the raw courage and power of
his predecessors. So too would he like to have the
opportunity to overcome his enemies, dominating
all those who do not adhere to his authority. By the
same token, he knows that he is a weak man and
that he resorts to cruelty only in order to gain mastery
over others. It is not clear in the story whether it is
the baron who ordered the count's stables to be set
on fire. Whatever the facts, Baron Metzengerstein
is under the influence of the horse archetype, and
when in its power, experiences a weakening of his
thinking capacity. The numinosity of the horse im-

age so overpowers his rational faculties that turbulence and chaos prevail, creating a condition favorable to psychokinesis.

Psychokinesis is still an unresolved mystery.
Such parapsychological happenings have been in-
vestigated by many researchers, including C. G.
Jung, who believed in the existence of a factor that
mediates between the apparent incommensurability
of body and psyche; it is this element which endows
matter with a kind of "psychic" faculty and the psyche with a sort of "materiality," enabling one to influence the other. That the physical body affects the
psyche is today a truism; so too is the reverse. If the
latter is true, it implies that "living matter has a
psychic aspect, and the psyche has a physical aspect."[26] To purse this logic even further, it might be
stated that reality in general is "grounded on an as
yet unknown substrate possessing material and at
the same time psychic qualities."[27] There are then
acausal correspondences linking psychic events and
physical events, and psychokinesis is one of them,
fusing the physical with the psychic.[28]

The fire image (the burning of the stables and
of the castle at the conclusion) is vital to Poe's tale
and reinforces the high-energy intensity of the narrative. Fire is fluid and spreads rapidly. It lights and
also illuminates; it warms and encourages vegetation
and growth; it also destroys, sears, and blinds. In
Poe's tale, the feeling is negative and revolves
strictly around anger, hatred, and rage—an urge to
conquer and kill.

As Metzengerstein rides his steed day in and day
out, he becomes one with the animal, yielding to
the powerful electric charges of this instinctual force
which wreaks havoc within his brain. That fire
breaks out in the castle shows the intensity of the

friction involved. Only by burning himself up in the castle will his uncontrollable warlike passions be consumed and destroyed.

The last vision of Metzengerstein rising upward on a cloud of smoke indicates the consummation but also an ascension, a sublimation of the flaming feelings of a psychotic individual. Examples of such imagery are replete in religious stories: Bellerophon, the Greek hero, attempted to ride to heaven on Pegasus, and Muhammad rode on his steed directly to heaven. The vision of the horse—that single archetypal emblem—is retained by the mind's eye as a kind of epiphany.

"The Colloquy of Monos and Una" (1841)

This allegorical fantasy enabled Poe to deal with the concepts of reincarnation and synesthesia, a sensation by which the hearing of a certain sound induces the visualization of a certain color; in it he also expressed his philosophical and artistic credo.

Una, meaning "the one" (the name Hawthorne gave his daughter), asks her lover, Monos, "the single one" about reincarnation. He cannot of course answer her question, he tells her, until he has died. But he does criticize the human race's naive belief in progress; the cities it has created have cut people off from nature and divested them of a sense of belonging. A century passes—both are now dead—before Una talks with Monos again. And Monos describes his sensations shortly after having passed into transition: He had felt as if he were awakening from a deep sleep, but aware of everything around him, yet divested of all volition. In time, a sixth sense began functioning, immersing him into a timeless sphere where he felt he had lost his individuality and merged with eternity. All seemed to fade. The void grew, and with it a "nebulous light had been extinguished."

Dust had returned to dust. The worms had food no more. The sense of being had at length utterly departed, and there reigned in its stead—instead of all things—dominant and perpetual—the autocrats *Place* and *Time*. For *that* which *was not*—for that which had no form—for that which had no thought—for that which had no sentience—for that which was soulless, yet of which matter formed no portion—for all this nothingness, yet for all this immortality, the grave was still a home, and the corrosive hours comates (p. 289).

As envisaged in "The Colloquy of Monos and Una," death is no longer a devouring gaping maw, as it was in Poe's shadow tales. Here it is described as a welcome, gentle, and comforting experience, a return to Mother Earth, an archetype that embraces those in need of comfort, warming the weary and cold. Monos rejects the world of contingencies which enslaves and commercialism which debases, in favor of the primal, timeless reality that unfolds in death. For Poe as for Novalis, death is seen only as an expansion of the universe one knows in sleep, whether naturally, hypnotically, or narcotically induced, a slow withdrawal from the world of multiplicity to one of unity.

After Monos has departed from the world of the living, he experiences a fusion of the senses: taste, smell, sight, touch, hearing are all blended into one "abnormal and intense" sentiment which allows him to be swept into the world around him, to experience it in all its vivid and variegated manifestations. Under such conditions, perceptions are vivified and recollections take on reality.

Synesthesia may be looked upon as a psychic awakening, a flaring of forces within the unconscious. It enables simultaneity of sense impressions. The symbolist poets—Baudelaire, Rimbaud, and Mallarmé—experienced it; it allowed them to penetrate the oneness of the cosmos, which brings harmony of being. Mystics, such as Jakob Boehme and Isaac Luria, knew synesthesia during moments of religious ecstasy when their souls seemed to ascend into the transpersonal realm, discovering therein the treasures that later were clustered in their apocalyptic writings.

Death for Swedenborg and Poe did not mean a cutting off from life. On the contrary, it implied a deeper concern, a cohabitation on another level of matter, another intensity of electric charges. Death and life are a matter of "a threshold of perception," writes Marie Louise von Franz, and belong to an area of existence that humans cannot yet understand because the energy intensity is superior to any that now can be comprehended or perceived.[29] After Mono's death he is no longer limited to the empirical sphere, not even to the intellectual domain, but en route to a spiritual area that transcends place and time.

"The Gold-Bug" (1843)

This is one of the most popular tales of Poe's. It deals with a synchronistic event that allows a search for hidden treasure to end successfully.

The narrator, a resident of Charleston, South Carolina, goes to visit an old friend, William Legrand, who lives with his aged black servant, Jupiter, on Sullivan's Island near Charleston's harbor. He finds Legrand elated because he had just found a rare species of *scarabaeus*. Although he has lent the insect to a friend for further scientific examination, he describes its brilliant gold color, its two jet-black spots near one end of its back and another at the other. He makes a sketch of the beetle for the narrator and hands it to him; the narrator inadvertently drops it on the floor near the hearth. Later he picks it up, and what he sees in no way resembles Legrand's description. He shows it to Legrand, who looks puzzled and then slips the piece of paper into his wallet. A month later the narrator, Legrand, and Jupiter go off to the desolate area where the insect had been found. Legrand follows a secret plan. He has Jupiter climb a certain tree, crawl out to its seventh branch, and drop the gold bug through the left eye of the skull that he finds fastened near the end of this branch.

The narrative thus far revolves around the virtually unique specimen, *scarabaeus caput hominis* of the gold bug, Poe writes. Scarabs possess a numinous power for the protagonist who is obsessed with his finding and for what he believes it can yield. In Poe's tale the scarab, a masculine symbol, is an energetic factor. Discovered in a wooded area, it symbolizes nature in its primitive and wild aspects.

That the *scarabaeus* is golden in color indicates the purity of its content. For the mystic and alchemist, gold has always represented supreme values: light, sun, and divine intelligence. It is not, however, visible, nor may such an entity be possessed by anyone.

Complex mathematical computations were in order before Legrand even arrived at the woodland spot where he first discovered the *scarabaeus*. He understood full well that the treasure identified with the *scarabaeus*, or gold bug, would be difficult to locate. He had Jupiter follow the instructions: walk out on the seventh branch of the tree and so forth. He saw where the left eye landed, dug a huge hole, but found nothing. Then Legrand realizes that a mistake has been made. He queries Jupiter and discovers he has mistakenly dropped the bug through the wrong eye. Legrand indicates the area where he must dig. This time he finds thousands of dollars in gold coin and many precious jewels.

How did Legrand know about the treasure? Why was there a disparity between his description of the *scarabaeus* and the narrator's? That the treasure beneath the earth could be discovered only by climbing a tree indicated that high and low are linked. The universe is one, and all else flows from this single source and reenters into it during the transformatory process. As for the tree, representing humanity's relationship with the cosmos—described in the scriptures as the Tree of Life and the Tree of Knowledge of Good and Evil—it also links the three aspects of worldly existence: the underground with its roots, the existential sphere with its trunks, and the spiritual domain with its branches which reach out into the air.

The skull and the eye are factors involved in the quest. In Plato's *Timaeus*, it said that "the human head is the image of the world," and it is by means of this spherical sphere that oneness is achieved and that supreme knowledge may be experienced. The fact that the *scarabaeus* must be dropped though the left eye rather than the right is also significant. The right side in myths and religious texts frequently has been identified with the rational aspect, the predictable and logical sphere. The left, *sinistra*, is believed to stand for the unconscious and unpredictable side of one's being, the side of the heart and of emotions which reacts to affects. Danger lurks here since no one knows how impulses will force one to behave. That Jupiter made an error and dropped the scarab through the right rather than the left eye indicates that without involving the whole of man, without tapping the transpersonal sphere of improbabilities, a treasure cannot be found. The eye, as we have already seen, is a symbol of great importance to Poe. It is the mirror of the soul, the sacred fire, man's intelligence. It is the eye's mission, according to certain ancient coffin texts, to protect the gods against violence as well as to ensure safe passage from one world to the next.

A combination of devices and forces was used by Legrand to reach his goal, and he explains how he arrived at his conclusions. When the narrator showed him the drawing that differed so markedly from the insect he originally had sketched, he understood that the heat of the hearth had revealed a secret message on the parchment. He deciphered its meaning: that a skull or death's-head is a piratical symbol. Since he was an amateur cryptologist, he understood that the various steps described would lead him to the treasure. The skull, he reasoned, was that of the sailor who had helped Captain Kidd bury the chest, after which Kidd bludgeoned him to death to make certain the secret would never be divulged. Only after the synchronistic event—the inexplicable coincidence which revealed the secret message— did Legrand realize that a treasure had been buried there. The timeless world makes known its directives in strange ways; only those attuned to its mysteries can discover its secret.

"Mesmeric Revelation" (1844)

This is one of the strangest and most eerie of all Poe's tales. The question posed at the outset concerns the possibility of hypnotizing someone to the point where the hypnotized person appears to be dead. The narrator, claims that it is impossible. Yet he agrees to hypnotize Vankirk, a friend now dying of tuberculosis, whom he has often before put in a trance in order to find out whether the soul is immortal. Under hypnosis the question-and-answer period begins. Vankirk states that God is the beginning of everything, that God is matter, and then goes on to explain what he means:

He [God] is not spirit, for he exists. Nor is he matter, *as you understand it.* But there are *gradations* of matter of which man knows nothing; the grosser impelling the finer, the finer pervading the grosser. The atmosphere, for example, impels the electric principle, while the electric principle permeates the atmosphere. These gradations of matter increase in rarity or finess, until we arrive at a matter *unparticled*—without particles—indivisible—*one*; and here the law of impulsion and permeation is modified. The ultimate, or unparticled matter, not only permeates all things but impels all things—and thus *is* all things within itself. This matter is God. What men attempt to embody in the word "thought" is this matter in motion (p. 428).

Poe enunciates a similar concept in *Eureka,* but in far greater detail, defining God as unparticled matter, an idea dear to him during the last decade of his life.

At the conclusion of the tale, the narrator, arousing Vankirk, notices "a bright smile irradiating all his features," and immediately afterward, Vankirk falls back dead. The narrator is left to wonder whether his friend had spoken to him from death's domain or from the land of the living.

Hypnotism has been practiced by occultists since ancient times. In the seventeenth century, J. B. van Helmont believed that "material nature draws her forms through constant magnetism from above" and that "there is established a free and mutual intercourse," whereupon "the whole is contained in

an individual."[30] Man has the power, particularly
when asleep, to direct the subtle fluid which runs
through the universe as he sees fit, thus connecting
himself with the corporeal and incorporeal world
and diffusing himself in it, as does light. Swedenborg
accepted many of the views of previous occultists,
to which he added his own belief that interaction
exists between our present world and the spirits of
the dead.

The body communicates with others which are about it
through the body, and the spiritual influence diffuses itself
chiefly through the hands, because these are the most
outward or *ultimum* of man; and through him, as in the
whole of nature, the first is contained in the last, as the
cause in the effect. The whole soul and the whole body
are contained in the hands as a medium of influence.[31]

The condition known as hyperesthesia, an extreme increase of the perceptive faculties which
frequently occurs during hypnotic states, maximizes
the potency of a person's senses. The slightest suggestion therefore is felt by the subject under hypnosis and is immediately communicated to some
obscure stratum of his or her unconscious to an intuitive or other subtle level that normal consciousness cannot reach. Scientists still do not understand
whether the senses are sharpened under hypnosis
or whether such a condition is the result of a state
of cerebral dissociation, allowing them to operate in
a relatively free manner.

"The Facts in the Case of M. Valdemar" (1845)

Here Poe deals not only with hypnosis but with an
even more fantastic subject, the question of sus-
pending death or life. It is a tale that created a sen-

sation in Europe; so much so that when Elizabeth
Barrett Browning did not find it included in her collection of Poe's tales, she was upset. The facts of the
story, she wrote later, had thrown her and her friends
into the "most admired disorder," or dreadful doubt
as to "whether it can be true." What so impressed
her was Poe's extraordinary ability of "making horrible improbabilities seem near and familiar."[32]

That a person could be kept alive after having
seemed to be dead has intrigued many, including
in our own time Walt Disney, who asked that his
body be frozen once he was pronounced dead so
that centuries later he might be revived in a world
more advanced in medical technology; thus he could
be cured of the disease that afflicted him.

The narrator in "The Facts in the Case of M.
Valdemar" is a mesmerist whose friend Ernest Valdemar is dying of turberculosis. The latter agrees to
be hypnotized just before his death and some ten
days later the narrator is summoned to do this in the
presence of doctors. The séance begins. Valdemar
heaves a deep sigh, stops rolling his eyes, and appears to be in a complete trance. He responds to
commands, and when the narrator questions him,
he opens his eyes. The following day, however, his
skin has turned a cadaverous color; his jaw has fallen,
and his mouth reveals a black and swollen tongue
which vibrates when he informs those present that
he is dead. No breath, no blood pressure, there is
no motion in his arms. Valdemar remains in this
condition for seven months. One Friday, the narrator
decides to awaken him by hypnotic passes. Suddenly, a yellow ichor of offensive odor flows from
his eyelids. When the hypnotist demands an expla-
nation, Valdemar turns red-cheeked and begs to be
awakened. His will is done; meanwhile, the hypnotist hears the word "dead," after which Valdemar's
"whole frame at once—within the space of a single

minute, or even less, shrunk—crumbled—absolutely rotted away beneath my hands. Upon the bed, before that whole company, there lay a nearly liquid mass of loathsome—of detestable putridity."

Mesmer, as has been mentioned, believed that he had discovered a new vitalistic force, a magnetic fluid which streamed from his hands into the patient's body, empowering him to subdue whatever troubled the patient or merely to put him to sleep. Experiments in divination, clairvoyance, and reactivation of unconscious persons or attempts to maintain life through hypnosis were the source of speculation in the eighteenth and nineteenth centuries and also the subjects of scientific investigation. Poe, familiar with such literature, knew that when a hypnotist stares into the eyes of a patient or makes mesmeric passes over the limbs, peculiar sensations invade the patient's being who may then experience a crisis.

To be able to converse with the dead through hypnosis, to question their sensations or whatever the experience, has been mankind's urge to know ever since the notion of death was confronted; it is a refusal to consider death as an end to life. The practice of necromancy was carried on in Greece. In the course of certain religious mysteries, initiates went down to Hades, symbolically speaking, to consult the dead. During the Middle Ages and Renaissance communication with the dead was considered sorcery and punished by death. Martinez de Pasqually and Claude de Saint-Martin, both eighteenth-century masons, claimed to have contacted the dead. Each in his own way influenced the romantic poets and novelists: Balzac, Hugo, Nerval, and Gautier. Hugo, after he exiled himself on the island of Guernsey, held séances and spoke with Socrates, Plato, Shakespeare, and other great minds.

Poe believed in the possibility of communicat-

ing with the dead, which was perhaps vital to his
well-being. Occult practices such as suspended animation intrigued him since they too could stay life
and retard death. To place his material as narrated
in "The Facts in the Case of M. Valdemar" in a scientific perspective, he calls upon doctors to witness
the experiment, which impressed the reading public.

Although the narrator states that as far as he
knows there has been no case on record that a dead
man has been hypnotized and kept in this condition
after death, this does not prevent him from probing
the question. He reasons that since Valdemar had a
nervous temperament, he could very easily experience hyperelectric charges which the hypnotist
would focus on him, and so activate the central
nervous system indefinitely. Just as people believe
in miracles, extraordinary events in which some
higher force intervenes in human affairs, so Poe also
felt the question of suspended animation to be a
possibility. After all, credence is given to the doc-
trines of resurrection, reincarnation, and virgin birth,
then why not to suspended animation?

"Some Words with a Mummy" (1845)

A cataleptic trance is the theme in "Some Words
with a Mummy." The narrator is asked by Dr. Ponnonner of the City Museum to attend a special re-
ception in honor of a mummy brought from Libya.
Scientists are present as the outer coverings of the
mummy are removed. They observe that the teeth,
hair, and fingernails are all in good condition. The
eyes appear to be glass. The brain and entrails have
not been removed. They begin their experiments
and apply electricity on the mummy without ex-
pecting any results. Suddenly, however, the leg

muscles begin to move. Dr. Ponnonner tweaks the mummy's nose, and it too moves; then it blinks its eyes, sneezes, and starts to talk in Egyptian. He explains that he has been asleep for so many years and that he is a victim of catalepsy. His contemporaries believed him to be dead and mummified him in the usual manner, but since he belonged to the Scarabaeus family, considered sacred, he was neither disemboweled nor debrained; he remained in a sleeping state. He is glad to know that such things can happen because it is important to correct the many historical errors that have been made. He discusses, for example, the creation and Adam, who generated spontaneously from the "red earth." And, he says, every time people bring up what they consider to be a novel subject such as phrenology, magnetism, astronomy, steel, railroads, steam, and other novelties, he cites examples of these very same things in ancient Egypt. The narrator leaves. Disgusted with his life, his times, and his wife, he asks to be embalmed. He would really like to know who will be president in 2045.

Magnetism, practiced in the temples of Isis, Osiris, and Serapis in ancient Egypt, was considered a curative agent, able to rid the sick of their diseases. In *The Book of the Dead* (chap. 125), a dialogue takes place between Osiris and an aspiring soul in which occult information is revealed to the questioner. These mysteries would help him survive the grueling transformatory ritual between life and death—and perhaps even retard death.[33]

It is not surprising that Poe referred to the ancient Egyptians and their cult of the dead, their god Osiris, for example, who descended into the underworld where he was reborn in the form of his son Horus, who in turn was resurrected as an earth force, spreading fertility throughout the land. Death for the

Egyptians was a prelude to life, a condition of eternal becoming. In Poe's story too, the mummy, though not dead, suffers from catalepsy and a suspension of his vital functions, including an insensibility to pain. Some psychiatrists today believe that catalepsy is a symptom that indicates an unconscious desire for death and a rejection of life. Catalepsy, it also has been posited, may be motivated or brought on by a desire to forget, to wipe out pain or an intolerable situation, to sleep undisturbed—eternally.[34]

Poe was an unrelenting delver into the soul, searching into man's collective past and hoping to find some sense of security for himself, which would bring serenity to his life.

"The Power of Words" (1845)

"The Power of Words" narrates a visionary experience that takes the reader into the sphere of both the living and the dead. Oinos, who has recently died, is discussing ontological questions with his friend Agathos: subjects such as mind, matter, and happiness in the world of the dead. What is most arresting in this dialogue is the definition given to happiness. Oinos suggested that happiness could be known when an individual became cognizant of all things. Agathos corrects the impression: "Ah, not in knowledge is happiness, but in the acquisition of knowledge."

The notion of words as matter then is brought up. The cosmos is filled with vibrating elements, Agathos declares: "No thought can perish," nor can there be any act without infinite repercussions. Each time one moves one's hand, impulses are generated and eternally actuated. All matter is influenced "upward and downward forever in their mortifications of old forms" or in their creation of new ones. Even words have "physical power"; every word is "an impulse on the air."

For the mystic and for Poe as well, all phenomena are a manifestation of but a single and ultimate reality that Buddhists call Dharmakaya (the Body of Being); Hindus, Brahma; Taoists, Tao; romantics, the all or being. This cosmic force transcends human concepts and is implicit in the incessant and eternal cosmic flow.

For the Eastern mystics, everything perceived by the senses—the word as well—is connected and experienced as a different aspect or varied manifestation of the same ultimate reality. Nature for the Hindu and the Buddhist is not divided; each manifestation of matter or nonmatter undergoes perpetual change in a dynamic which incorporates time and change. The cosmos—and Poe shared this view—is considered an "inseparable reality—forever in motion, alive, organic."[35]

Words are objects in the same way that thoughts or feelings are. Both are part of motion and change, an element of time—an energetic quality—mass. As Einstein's theory of relativity posited $E = mc^2$ (c being the speed of light), any particle, subatomic or supergalactic, transcends the very notion of polarities and goes beyond the concept of existence and nonexistence. It introduces a fresh way of thought that encourages scientists and psychologists as well to alter their past, limited mental habits. Words reveal Poe's unquenchable thirst for knowledge.

In *Eureka*, Poe declared that like matter, which is forever being agitated and stirred by "seemingly gyrating, or vortical movements" and transformed into "converting charges of energy," so too words are electrically charged; they attract and repel not only by the impact of their intellectual or sensual meanings but as electromagnetic phenomena.

When Poe speaks of the power of words, he is in effect indicating their force in terms of mass and velocity, their multidimensional influences or impressions on phenomena within their range and intensity. Words then have physical sound waves, "a vibrational pattern in space and time," as particles, whose motion may be described in terms of "its velocity and its energy in motion."[36] For the poet, words are also mobile, catalysts that arouse power, impulse, and force, living and dynamic. They both create and destroy emotion; they grate and grind or lull and cradle.

Words for Poe were physical entities—matter—which brought him to the edge of an abyss, a maelstrom or mountain peak, a vantage point that allowed him to explore the strange creatures that he projected about him—anima and shadow—and to investigate the natural and cosmic worlds in all their ramifications. They brought him happiness in the very process of acquiring knowledge. Words were feeling forces for Poe, his companions in his loneliness.

5

Conclusion

Poe is a phenomenon unique in literature. Delving into questions that preoccupied his contemporaries, he tantalizes us still today. His tales and detective stories, the worlds of the occult and parapsychological which he conjures up before us, the domain of psychogenic and psychosomatic illness—that whole pathological dimension—come to life under his aegis. Poe also encapsulates in his works those polarities which hounded him: the empirical and spiritual worlds. These seemingly incompatible domains are meticulously structured in his tales: each is wrought in great detail, and each searches through the rubble of the lives he brings to his readers for insights, for ways to right a wrong, to balance the warped, harmonize conflict, and discover truth. That Poe is drawn to horror and the morbid and was also fascinated by scientific and metaphysical problems indicates his deep need to break out of the constricting environment in which he found himself, the social structure and the limited, pragmatic outlook of his times. Yet there was an equally powerful drive within him, based on psychological and emotional needs, to remain in a circumscribed and closed world. The need for love and companionship was primal in Poe as was his sense of severance from a public that never understood his work and which rejected him and turned its back on his great literary achievements. Poe's uncontrollable tension perhaps catalyzed his creative urge. Loneliness forced him to speak out, and to disclose the macabre depths raging within him. He was a man of solitude; yet he could not be silenced.

Whatever the area Poe chose to explore in his tales, each was presented with finesse, artistry, and great sensitivity, often also with deep emotion. His poems, particularly those focusing on youthful lost love, sing out their music from the heart and are indeed timeless. They answer a longing in everyone to know or to remember how to love and be loved. They strike a responsive note in all those who listen to these marvelous lyrical creations. Poe's tales, revolving around turbulent storms and maelstroms are descents into the personal and collective unconscious; they are rites of passage which open up vast areas within the subliminal realm. His feminine characters emerge from the same depths as skeletal anima figures—wraithlike females, sometimes listless, ill phantasmagorias, at other times active presences intent on acquiring more and more knowledge, the better to dominate the unsuspecting male. It is from these regions also that Poe's frightening destructive shadow beings come. The mystical tales take us out of our own limited existence into a world of fantasy and wonderment. Poe's powers of imagination seem virtually limitless in his revelations of extraterrestrial worlds: subterranean and supergalactic domains within and without the limits of the earth proper, immobilizing the reader as Poe recounts with verve—but always with extreme control—the lot of those living in silent spatial spheres, quiescent, astounded, and perplexed by that glowing mystery which is life itself.

Applicable to Poe is the statement made by

Thomas Mann in *Death in Venice*: "Solitude gives birth to the original in us, to beauty unfamiliar and perilous—to poetry. But also, it gives birth to the opposite: to the perverse, the illicit, the absurd."

Poe deeply immersed himself in his own interior world, and it is from those depths that he speaks to us today and holds us in his spell as artist and seer.

Notes

2. THE LIFE

1. *The Complete Works of Edgar Allan Poe*. Edited and with a Biography by James A. Harrison, p. 2. Said to a friend, F. W. Thomas.
2. Floyd Stovall, *Edgar Poe the Poet*, p. 157. From the "Review of *The Old Curiosity Shop*." *Graham's Magazine*, May 1841.
3. Agnes M. Bondurant, *Poe's Richmond*, p. 129. Written by Rachel to her brother, Samuel Mordecai of Richmond.
4. Harrison, p. 10.
5. Ibid., p. 18.
6. Bondurant, p. 19.
7. Ibid., pp. 139-40.
8. Harrison, p. 36.
9. Ibid., p. 39. Mr. Thomas Goode Tucker, a friend of Poe's at the University of Virginia.
10. Harrison, p. 47.
11. *The Letters of Edgar Allan Poe*. Edited by John Ward Ostrom, I, p. 7 (March 19, 1827).
12. Ibid., p. 9 (March 20, 1827).
13. Harrison, p. 77.
14. *Letters*, p. 29 (August 10, 1829).
15. Harrison, p. 102.
16. Bondurant, p. 184.
17. *Letters*, p. 69 (August 29, 1835).
18. Ibid., p. 71.

19. Harrison, p. 115.
20. *Literary Criticism of Edgar Allan Poe.* Edited by Robert L. Hough; "Hawthorne's *Twice-Told Tales*," *Graham's Magazine*, May 1842, pp. 133-41.
21. *The Complete Edgar Allan Poe Tales*, p. 246. All quotations from Poe's tales will be taken from this edition, pp. 246-48.
22. Harrison, p. 125.
23. *Letters*, II, p. 354 (Jan. 4, 1848).
24. *Letters*, I, p. 252 (April 7, 1844).
25. Ibid., p. 256 (July 2, 1844).
26. Harrison, p. 254. Mr. F. M. Hopkins described the home in *The Review of Reviews*, April 1896.
27. Harrison, p. 262.
28. Ibid., p. 263.
29. Ibid., p. 269.
30. Ibid., p. 293.
31. *Letters*, II, p. 414 (Jan. 11, 1849).
32. Harrison, p. 275.
33. *The Science Fiction of Edgar Allan Poe.* Edited by Harold Beaver; *Eureka*, pp. 397, 402.
34. *Letters*, II, p. 452 (July 7, 1849).
35. Harrison, p. 335.

3. THE POEMS

1. *The Letters of Edgar Allan Poe*, I (Oct.-November 1829), p. 32.
2. Ibid. (December 1, 1835), p. 79.
3. "The Philosophy of Composition," p. 368.
4. *Letters* (July 10, 1844), p. 260.
5. "The Philosophy of Composition," pp. 366, 388.
6. Ibid., p. 388.
7. *The Science Fiction of Edgar Allan Poe.* Edited by Harold Beaver; *Eureka*, p. 220.
8. Vincent Buranelli, *Edgar Allan Poe*, p. 46.
9. "The Poetic Principle," p. 389.
10. Edgar Allan Poe. *Selected Writings*. Edited by David Galloway, p. 396. From "Review of Poems by Drake

and Halleck," *Southern Literary Messenger*, II (April 1836), pp. 327-28.

11. "The Poetic Principle," p. 383.
12. "The Philosophy of Composition," p. 365.
13. *Letters* (Jan. 18, 1845), p. 378.
14. *Literary Criticism of Edgar Allan Poe.* Edited by Robert L. Hough, pp. 218-19; "Song Writing," *Southern Literary Messenger*, XV (April 1849).
15. *Letters* (July 2, 1844), p. 257.
16. Ibid.
17. "The Philosophy of Composition," p. 365.
18. "The Poetic Principle," p. 387.
19. Hough, p. 54. From "The Poetic Principle," *Sartain's Magazine*, VII (October 1850).
20. Ibid., pp. 95, 122. From "Broadway Journal," I (Jan. 11, 1845) and "Ballads and Other Poems," *Graham's Magazine*, XX (April 1842).
21. Ibid.
22. Ibid., p. 75. "Wordsworth and Coleridge," *Southern Literary Messenger*, II (July 1836).
23. *Collected Works of Edgar Allan Poe*, I. *Poems.* Edited by Thomas Ollive Mabbot, pp. 373-74. All the poems in this text are taken from this edition.
24. *The Science Fiction of Edgar Allan Poe*, p. xiv. "Mr. Griswold and the Poets," *Boston Miscellany* (November 1842).
25. Floyd Stovall, *Edgar Poe the Poet*, p. 109.
26. Hough, p. 8. "Song Writing," *Southern Literary Messenger*, XV (April 1849).
27. Poe, "Letter to B," 1831.
28. *Collected Works of Edgar Allan Poe*, I. *Poems*, pp. 373-4.
29. *Letters to Edgar Allan Poe*, I. Edited by J. W. Ostrom, p. 385.
30. Marie Louise von Franz, *Number and Time*, p. 19.
31. Erich Neumann, *The Origins and History of Consciousness*, p. 55.
32. *Collected Works of Edgar Allan Poe*, I. p. 351.
33. Dickens used a speaking bird, a talking raven, in *Barnaby Rudge*. Thomas Holly Chivers, the Georgia-

born physician (1809-58), a friend of Poe's, later ac-
cused him of plagiarizing his poem "To Allegra
Florence in Heaven" about the death of his daughter.
Poe's "The Raven" was influenced by Elizabeth
Barrett Browning's "Lady Geraldine's Courtship."
See *Collected Works of Edgar Allan Poe*, I, p. 356.
Poe dedicated his volume, *The Raven and Other
Poems* (1845), to Miss Barrett.

34. James A. Harrison, *A Biography*, p. 255.
35. Ibid.
36. Ibid.
37. "The Poetic Principle," p. 388.

4. THE TALES

1. "The Unknown Poe." From *A Rebours* by J. K.
   Huysmans, p. 110.
2. G. R. Thompson, *Poe's Fiction*, pp. 69–70; 106–108.
3. *Literary Criticism of Edgar Allan Poe*. Edited by
   Robert L. Hough, p. 130. From *Broadway Journal*,
   Oct. 4, 1845.
4. Ibid., *Graham's Magazine*, May 1842.
5. Edgar Allan Poe, "Tale-Writing—Twice-Told
   Tales—Mosses from an Old Manse. By Nathaniel
   Hawthorne," 1842.
6. Mircea Eliade, *Rites and Symbols*, p. 111.
7. Edward Edinger, "An Outline of Analytical Psychology," p. 12.
8. Ibid., p. 12.
9. Edgar Allan Poe, *Letters*, I p. 49.
10. "The Unknown Poe." From *A Rebours* by J. K.
    Huysmans, p. 111.
11. Henri Baruk, *L'hypnose*, p. 40.
12. Henri F. Ellenberger, *The Discovery of the Uncon-
    scious*, pp. 126, 245.
13. Marvin Spiegelman, "Psychology and the Occult,"
    Spring 1976, p. 136.
14. Ellenberger, p. 202.
15. Ibid., p. 159.

16. "The Unknown Poe." From *A Rebours* by J. K. Huysmans, p. 110.

17. Ellenberger, pp. 215-18.

18. Ibid., pp. 304-5.

19. Ibid., pp. 106; 78.

20. Ibid., p. 203.

21. Ibid., p. 170.

22. C. G. Jung, *Collected Works*, 8, p. 438; Arthur Koestler, *The Roots of Coincidence*, p. 93.

23. A. A. Roback and Thomas Kiernan, *Pictorial History of Psychology and Psychiatry*, pp. 189-202.

24. Agnes M. Bondurant, *Poe's Richmond*, p. 139.

25. Ellenberger, pp. 62-63.

26. Ibid., pp. 75-78.

27. Ibid.

28. C. G. Jung, *C. W.* 5, p. 281.

29. Marie Louise von Franz, "Archetypes Surrounding Death," *Quadrant*, Summer 1979, p. 45.

30. R. T. Clark, *Myth and Symbol in Ancient Egypt*, p. 93.

31. Lewis Spence, *An Encyclopaedia of Occultism*, p. 216.

32. Edgar Allan Poe, *Letters*, II, p. 320 (June 15, 1846).

33. Clark, p. 164.

34. C. G. Jung, *C. W.*, 18, p. 428.

35. Fritjof Capra, *The Tao of Physics*, p. 24.

36. Ibid., pp. 155-56.

Selected Bibliography

PRIMARY SOURCES:

The Science Fiction of Edgar Allan Poe. New York: Penguin Books, 1978. Edited by Harold Beaver. *Eureka*, etc.

The Unknown Poe. San Francisco, California: City Lights, 1980. Edited by Raymond Foye.

Edgar Allan Poe. Selected Writings. New York: Penguin Books, 1981. Edited by David Galloway. "The Philosophy of Furniture," etc.

Literary Criticism of Edgar Allan Poe. Lincoln, Nebraska: University of Nebraska Press, 1969. Edited by Robert L. Hough.

Collected Works of Edgar Allan Poe. I. *Poems*. Cambridge, Mass.: Harvard University Press, 1969. Edited by Thomas O. Mabbott.

Selected Poetry and Prose of Edgar Allan Poe. New York: The Modern Library, 1953. Edited by T. O. Mabbott. "Instinct vs Reason—A Black Cat," "R. W. Emerson," "The Philosophy of Composition," "The Poetic Principle," "Marginalia," etc.

The Complete Poems and Stories of Edgar Allan Poe. New York: Knopf, 1946. Edited by Arthur Hobson Quinn and Edward H. O'Neill.

The Complete Edgar Allan Poe Tales. New York: Avenel Books, 1981.

The Complete Poetry and Selected Criticism of Edgar Allan Poe. Edited by Allan Tate. New York: New American Library, 1981.

SECONDARY SOURCES:

Bittner, William. *Poe: A Biography*. Boston: Little, Brown and Co., 1962.

Bondurant, Agnes M. *Poe's Richmond*. Richmond, Virginia: Garret and Massie, Inc., 1942.

Buranelli, Vincent. *Edgar Allan Poe*. Boston, Mass.: Twayne Publishers, 1977.

Capra, Fritjof. *The Tao of Physics*. Berkeley, California: Shambhala, 1975.

Clark, R. T. Rundle. *Myth and Symbol in Ancient Egypt*. London: Thames and Hudson, 1978.

Davidson, Edward H. *Poe, A Critical Study*. Cambridge, Mass.: Harvard University Press, 1966.

Edinger, Edward. "An Outline of Analytical Psychology," unpublished.

Eliade, Mircea. *Shamanism*. Princeton, N.J.: Princeton University Press, 1964.

Ellenberger, Henri F. *The Discovery of the Unconscious*. New York: Basic Books, Inc., 1970.

Fagin, N. Bryllion. *The Histrionic Mr. Poe*. Baltimore, Md.: The Johns Hopkins Press, 1967.

Franz, Marie Louise von. "Archetypes Surrounding Death," *Quadrant*, Summer 1979.

Halliburton, David. *Edgar Allan Poe: A Phenomenological View*. Princeton, N.J.: Princeton University Press, 1973.

Harrison, James A. *The Complete Works of Edgar Allan Poe. Biography*. New York: Thomas Y. Crowell, 1902.

Jung, C. G. *Complete Works*. V. New York: Pantheon Books, 1956; X. New York: Pantheon Books, 1964; XVIII. Princeton, N.J.: Princeton University Press, 1976. All the volumes were translated by F. R. C. Hull.

Koestler, Arthur. *The Roots of Coincidence*. New York: Random House, 1972.

Krutch, Joseph Wood. *Edgar Allan Poe: A Study in Genius*. New York: Knopf, 1926.

Miller, John Carl. *Building Poe Biography*. Baton Rouge, Louisiana: Louisiana State University Press, 1977.

Pollin, Burton R. *Discoveries in Poe*. Notre Dame, Ind.: University of Notre Dame Press, 1977.

Regan, Robert. *Poe: A Collection of Critical Essays*. Englewood Cliffs, N.J.: Prentice-Hall, 1967.

Roback, A. A. and Thomas Kiernan. *Pictorial History of Psychology and Psychiatry*. New York: The Philosophical Library, 1969.

Spence, Lewis. *An Encyclopaedia of Occultism*. Secaucus, N.J.: The Citadel Press, 1974.

Spiegelman, Marvin. "Psyche and the Occult," *Spring*, 1976.

Stovall, Floyd. *Edgar Poe the Poet*. Charlottesville, Virginia: University of Virgina Press, 1969.

Thompson, G. R. *Poe's Fiction*. Madison, Wisconsin: University of Wisconsin Press, 1974.

Wagenknecht, Edward. *Edgar Allan Poe*. New York: Oxford University Press, 1963.

Works of Plato. Jowett Translation. New York: Tudor Publishing Co., n. d.

Index